Adobe® Photoshop® *elements* 3.0

CLASSROOM IN A BOOK®

www.adobepress.com

Adobe

Contents

Getting Started

Adobe® Photoshop® Elements 3.0 for Windows® delivers image-editing tools that balance power and versatility with ease of use. Photoshop Elements 3.0 is ideal for home users, hobbyists, business users, and professional photographers—anyone who wants to produce good-looking pictures and sophisticated graphics for the Web and for print.

If you've used earlier versions of Photoshop Elements, you'll find that this *Classroom in a Book®* teaches many advanced skills and innovative features that Adobe Systems introduces in this version. If you're new to Adobe Photoshop Elements 3.0, you'll learn the fundamental concepts and techniques that help you master the application.

About Classroom in a Book

Adobe Photoshop Elements 3.0 Classroom in a Book is part of the official training series for Adobe graphics and publishing software developed by Adobe Systems experts. Each lesson in this book is made up of a series of self-paced projects that give you hands-on experience using Photoshop Elements 3.0.

The *Classroom in a Book* is a little like a cross between a cookbook and a text book. No cookbook describes every possible recipe or kind of kitchen equipment. But, when you follow the step-by-step instructions and see the results, you can learn a lot about cooking—or, in this case, about working with digital images in Photoshop Elements 3.0.

Unlike a cookbook, the *Adobe Photoshop Elements 3.0 Classroom in a Book* provides all the ingredients for the projects. You'll find the complete set of image files needed for the projects on the CD attached to the inside back cover of this book.

Prerequisites

Before you begin working on the lessons in this book, make sure that you and your computer are ready. The next two topics describe how to determine that you're properly set up to begin working with Photoshop Elements 3.0.

The lessons in this book are designed to be used only on Windows 2000 or Windows XP. Some files, steps, and descriptions in this book won't apply to Adobe Photoshop Elements 3.0 for Macintosh.

Requirements on your computer

You'll need about 150 MB of free space on your hard disk for the lesson files and the work files you'll create. The lesson files are on the CD attached to the inside back cover of this book. These image files are necessary for your work in the lessons.

Required skills

The lessons in the *Adobe Photoshop Elements 3.0 Classroom in a Book* assume that you have a working knowledge of your computer and its operating system. This book does not teach the most basic and generic computer skills. If you can answer *yes* to the following questions, then you're probably well qualified to start working on the projects in these lessons. Most users should do the lessons in the order they occur in the book.

• Do you know how to use the Microsoft Windows Start button and the Windows taskbar? Can you open menus and submenus, and choose items on those menus?

• Do you know how to use My Computer, Windows Explorer, or Internet Explorer to find items stored in folders on your computer?

• Are you comfortable using the mouse to move the pointer, select items, drag, and deselect? Have you used context menus (sometimes called *shortcut menu*), which open when you right-click items?

• When you have two or more open applications, do you know how to switch from one to another? Do you know how to switch to the Windows desktop?

• Do you know how to open, close, and minimize individual windows? Can you move them to different locations on your screen? Can you resize a window (by dragging)?

• Can you scroll (vertically and horizontally) to see the rest of the document or page?

• Are you familiar with the menus across the top of an application and how to use it?

• Have you used dialog boxes, such as the Print dialog box? Do you know how to click arrow icons to open a pop-up menu within a dialog box?

• Can you open, save, and close a file? Are you familiar with word processing tasks, such as typing, selecting words, backspacing, deleting, copying, pasting, and changing text?

• Do you know how to open and find information in Microsoft Windows Help?

If there are gaps in your mastery of these skills, see the Microsoft documentation for your version of Windows. Or, ask a computer-savvy friend or your instructor for help.

Installing Adobe Photoshop Elements 3.0

You must purchase the Adobe Photoshop Elements 3.0 software separately and install it on a computer running Windows 2000 or Windows XP. For system requirements and complete instructions on installing the software, see the *InstallReadMe* file on the Photoshop Elements 3.0 application CD.

Note: *Have your serial number handy before you start to install the application; you can find the serial number on the registration card or CD sleeve for the application. You do not need a serial number to copy the lesson files from the* Classroom in a Book *CD.*

Copying the Classroom in a Book files

The CD attached to the inside back cover of this book includes all the electronic files for these lessons. Because the files will be organized with a catalog that is an essential part of many projects, keep all the files on your computer until you finish all the lessons.

Note: *The images on the CD are practice files, provided for your personal use in these lessons. You are not authorized to use these photographs commercially, or to publish or distribute them in any form without written permissions from Adobe Systems, Inc., and the individual photographers who took the pictures or other copyright holders.*

Copying the Lessons files from the CD

1 Insert the *Adobe Photoshop Elements 3.0 Classroom in a Book* CD in your CD-ROM drive. If a message appears asking what you want Windows to do, select Open Folder To View Files Using Windows Explorer, and click OK.

If no message appears, open My Computer and double-click the CD icon to open it.

2 Locate the Lessons folder on the CD and copy it to the My Documents folder on your computer.

3 When your computer finishes copying the Lessons file, remove the CD from your CD-ROM drive and put it away.

Go on to the procedure below before you start the lessons.

Creating a catalog

You'll use a catalog to organize the image files for the lessons in this book. This keeps all of your images together in one easy-to-access location. You'll use this process whenever you need to import images into Photoshop Elements from your digital camera or images already stored on your hard drive.

1 Start Adobe Photoshop Elements. In the Photoshop Elements start screen choose View and Organize Photos. This starts Photoshop Elements in the Organizer mode

2 Choose File > Catalog and in the Catalog window that opens, click the New button. Enter the file name **CIB Catalog** and then click the Save button.

3 Choose File > Get Photos > From Files and Folders. In the Get Photos from Files and Folders window, navigate to the My Documents folder. Click only once to select the Lessons folder that you copied from the CD. Do not double-click, as you do not want to open then Lessons folder. Confirm the Get Photos from Subfolders checkbox is selected in the lower right corner of the window, and then click the Get Photos button.

4 The Import Attached Tags window opens. Click the Select All button, and then click the OK button. These images contain additional information, known as tags, that will help you organize them as you proceed through the book.

After the image files are imported into the catalog, the tags are displayed along the right side of the display. These will be referenced in the lessons later in the book.

5 Photoshop Elements displays a dialog box, informing you that the only items displayed in the Organizer are those you just imported. Click OK to close this window.

Additional resources

Adobe Photoshop Elements Classroom in a Book is not meant to replace documentation that comes with the program or to be a comprehensive reference for every feature in Photoshop Elements 3.0 for Windows. For additional information about program features, refer to any of these resources:

• Photoshop Elements Help, which is built into the Adobe Photoshop Elements 3.0 application. You can view it by choosing Help > Photoshop Elements Help.

• The Adobe website (www.adobe.com), which you can view by choosing Help > Photoshop Elements Online. You can also choose Help > Online Support for access to the support pages on the Adobe website. Both require that you have Internet access.

• The *Adobe Photoshop Elements 3.0 Getting Started Guide*, which is included either in the box with your copy of Adobe Photoshop Elements 3.0 or on the installation CD for the application software in PDF format. If you don't already have Adobe Reader (or if you have an older version of Adobe Acrobat Reader) installed on your computer, you can install a current version from the installation CD, or download a free copy from the Adobe website (www.adobe.com).

Adobe Certification

The Adobe Training and Certification Programs are designed to help Adobe customers improve and promote their product-proficiency skills. The Adobe Certified Expert (ACE) program is designed to recognize the high-level skills of expert users. Adobe Certified Training Providers (ACTP) use only Adobe Certified Experts to teach Adobe software classes. Available in either ACTP classrooms or on-site, the ACE program is the best way to master Adobe products. For Adobe Certified Training Programs information, visit the Partnering with Adobe website at http://partners.adobe.com.

Reconnecting missing files to a catalog

The relationship between the images and a catalog depends on the folder structure on your computer and the location of the image files that are a part of the catalog. If you move the Lessons folder or any of the files after you have created the catalog, you may need to reconnect the files. This procedure is only necessary if you move the Lesson files and Photoshop Elements alerts you that it can not find an image file. If your lesson files have not been moved, or you have not received an alert message regarding missing files, you do not need to follow this procedure and can go on to the next lesson.

Moving or renaming a catalogued image file or folder can break the catalog connections. Fortunately, reconnecting them is easy. If you ever receive a message that individual files can not be located, simply complete the following steps:

1 Choose File > Reconnect > All Missing Files. If a message appears, "There are no files to find," click OK, and then skip the rest of this procedure. Your files do not need to be reconnected.

2 If a message appears, "Searching for missing files," click the Browse button. The Reconnect Missing Files dialog box opens. On the Browse tab on the right side of the dialog box, use the upper area to find and open the Lessons folder. Locate and select the folder that has the same name as the folder located underneath the small picture, on the left side of the dialog box.

3 Select the folder with the same name as the folder underneath the thumbnail image on the left side of the window.

4 After you select the appropriate folder and the correct thumbnail picture appears in the right side of the dialog box, click the Reconnect button.

5 Continue selecting the appropriate folders and clicking the Reconnect button as you find matching files. When all the files are reconnected, click Close.

You can now use the Photoshop Elements Organizer to select and open files in the Photoshop Elements Editor.

Note: This procedure also eliminates error messages regarding missing files when you work with Creations or print from Organizer.

1 Getting and Organizing Photos

Organizer is a new component in Photoshop Elements 3.0. You'll learn key secrets to using Organizer in this lesson, whether you're a veteran of version 2.0 or new to Photoshop Elements. For many simple projects, the Organizer component may be all you need to get the job done.

In this lesson you will learn how to do the following:

- Open Adobe Photoshop Elements 3.0 in Organizer mode.

- Create a catalog of your images by gathering image file information in three ways.

- Import images from a digital camera or scanner onto your computer and into a catalog.

- Apply automatic fixes to photos to correct the most common problems.

- Crop a photo to include only the best part of the picture.

- Change the display of thumbnails in your catalog in numerous ways.

- Create, organize, and apply tags to images to help you search for them later.

Photoshop Elements 3.0 for Windows operates in two component parts: Editor and Organizer. These two interrelated sides work hand-in-hand to help you find, share, and make corrections in your photographs and images.

Before you start working in Adobe Photoshop Elements 3.0, make sure that you have installed Photoshop Elements 3.0 on your computer from the application CD. (See "Installing Adobe Photoshop Elements 3.0" on page 3.)

Also make sure that you have correctly copied the Lessons folder from the CD in the back of this book onto your computer hard disk. (See "Copying the Classroom in a Book files" on page 3.)

Most people need between one and two hours to complete all the projects in this lesson.

Getting started

In this lesson, you're going to work in only one of the twin components that make up Photoshop Elements 3.0. The Organizer side of Photoshop Elements 3.0 is new for this version. If you're familiar with Adobe Photoshop Album, you'll recognize the principle functions and features of Photoshop Elements Organizer.

1 Start Photoshop Elements, either by double-clicking the shortcut () on your desktop or by choosing Start > Programs > Adobe Photoshop Elements 3.0.

2 Do one of the following:

- If the Welcome screen appears, click View And Organize Photos in the row of shortcut buttons across the upper part of the Welcome window.

- If Photoshop Elements 3.0 (Editor) opens instead of the Welcome screen, click the Photo Browser button (⊘⃞) in the middle of the shortcuts bar across the upper part of the window. (It takes about 10 seconds for the Organizer component to load for the first time in a work session.)

- If Photoshop Elements 3.0 (Organizer) opens, you don't have to do anything more.

Getting photos

The Organizer component of Photoshop Elements 3.0 gives you a gathering place where you can efficiently organize, sort, and even do basic editing of your pictures. When you want to print your photographs or send them in e-mail, having the images collected in the Organizer is an essential step in the process, as you'll see later in this lesson.

Creating a new catalog

You organize your photographs in *catalogs*, which manage the image files on your computer but are independent of the photo files themselves. You can include video and audio files along with digital photographs and scans in your catalogs. A single catalog can efficiently handle thousands of photos, but you can also create separate catalogs for different types of work, to keep them separate. You'll do that now so that you won't confuse the practice files for this book with your own photographs and files.

1 In Photoshop Elements 3.0 (Organizer), choose File > Catalog.

Note: In this book, forward arrow character (>) is used to refer to commands and submenus for the menus at the top of the application window: File, Edit, and so forth.

2 In the Catalog dialog box, click New.

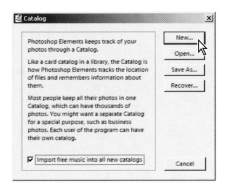

3 In the New Catalog dialog box, type **Lesson1** for File Name, and click Save without making any other changes in the settings.

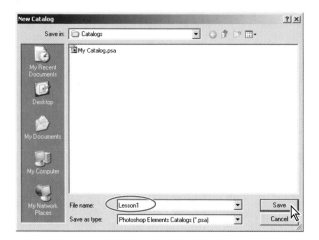

Now you have a special catalog that you'll use just for this lesson. All you need is some pictures to put in it.

Dragging photos from Windows Explorer

This method of adding photographs to a Photoshop Elements 3.0 Organizer catalog couldn't be easier or more intuitive. It uses the familiar drag-and-drop technique.

1 Minimize Photoshop Elements 3.0 Organizer by clicking the Minimize button (_) on the right side of the title bar. Or, click the application button on the Windows taskbar to minimize it.

2 Open My Computer by whatever method you usually use, such as double-clicking an icon on the desktop, using the Start menu, or using Windows Explorer.

Note: If you need help finding Windows Explorer or navigating the multi-leveled folder structure on your computer, see Windows Help (click Start and choose Help And Support).

3 Resize and arrange the My Computer window so that it does not fill the screen. Then reopen Organizer and resize it as needed so that you can see both of windows.

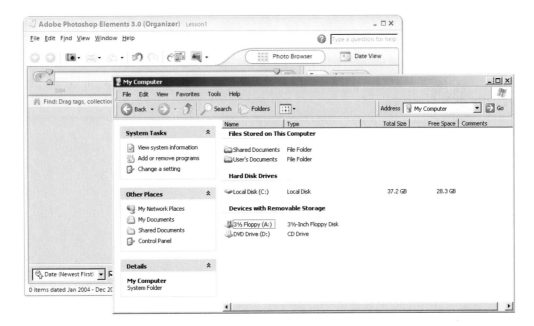

4 In My Computer, navigate the folder structure on your computer to find and open the Lessons folder that you copied and expanded, and then select and open the Lesson01 folder. (If you don't see the Lessons folder, see "Copying the Classroom in a Book files" on page 3.)

You'll see three folders inside the Lesson01 folder: Batch1, Batch2, and Batch3.

5 Drag the Batch1 folder into Organizer.

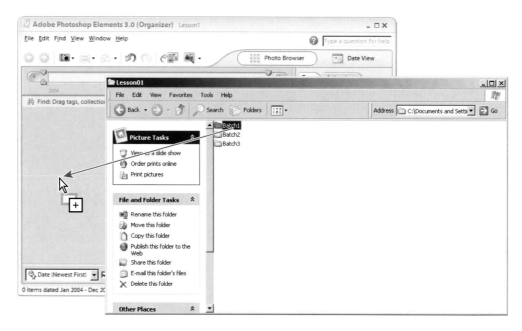

6 If a message appears, telling you that only the newly imported files will appear, click OK.

7 (Optional) Click the Maximize button (□) in the upper right corner of the Organizer window to allow the window to cover the entire screen.

You'll now see thumbnails of the four images you've added to your Lesson1 catalog. Don't drag the other two batches into Organizer because you're going to use different methods of adding them to your catalog.

Getting photos from specific locations

A second technique for adding photographs to your catalog is similar to the first one, but you use a menu instead of having to resize and arrange windows on the desktop.

1 Choose File > Get Photos > From Files And Folders.

2 In the Get Photos From Files And Folders dialog box, navigate to the Lessons\Lesson01 folder, and open the Batch2 folder.

3 One by one, select each of the five image files in the Batch2 folder, and look at the Preview area to see a thumbnail of each image.

Obviously, there are two identical copies of the photo of a tulip field, so you won't need to import both of them.

4 Select 01_05.jpg. Then hold down Shift and select 01_08.jpg to select the four images. Then click the Get Photos button.

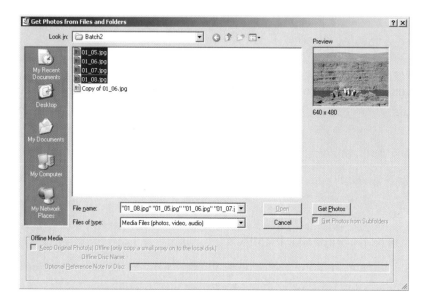

5 If a message appears about the imported items, click OK. Or, click the Don't Show Again option, and then click OK.

6 Click the Back To All Photos button above the thumbnails area to see all eight images.

Now, you have a total of eight images in your Lesson1 catalog. The thumbnails are arranged according to the date on which the image file was created, going from the newest to the oldest.

Searching for photos to add

This method is probably the one you'll want to use if you're not sure where in your folder structure you've stashed photographs and other resources over the years. Ordinarily, you might run this search on your entire hard disk or for the entire My Documents folder. For this demonstration, you'll limit your search area to a very restricted part of the folder organization on your computer.

1 In Photoshop Elements 3.0 Organizer, choose File > Get Photos > By Searching.

2 In the dialog box that appears, choose Browse from the Look In pop-up menu.

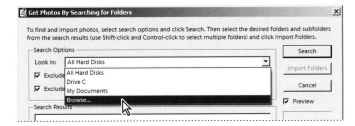

3 In the Browse For Folder dialog box, select the Lesson01 folder, and click OK.

4 Click the Search button.

5 In the Search Results, select only the Batch3 folder, and then click Import Folders.

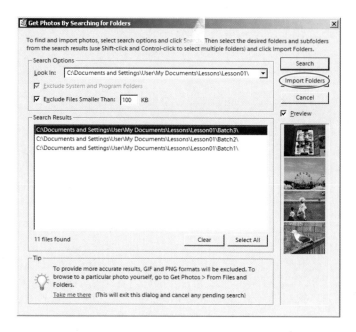

6 In Organizer, examine the four, newly imported image thumbnails, and then click Back To All Photos.

You now have 12 images to work with in this lesson.

Note: *Lesson 5 presents related topics about importing images from files in other formats. When you're ready, see "Project 1: Importing images from a PDF document" on page 173 and "Project 2: Importing still images from video" on page 174 in Lesson 5.*

Importing from a digital camera

This exercise is optional and requires that you have an available digital camera with pictures on it. You can either do this procedure now or wait until later, when you're ready to start doing your own projects in Photoshop Elements 3.0.

1 Connect your digital camera or the card reader for your digital camera to your computer following the instructions for your camera that came from the manufacturer.

2 Do one of the following:

• If the Get Photos From Camera Or Card Reader dialog box appears automatically, wait while Photoshop Elements collects information from your camera.

• If a different dialog box appears, click Cancel. Then, in Photoshop Elements Organizer, choose File > Get Photos > From Camera Or Card Reader. When the dialog box appears, select your camera or card reader in the Get Photos From pop-up menu.

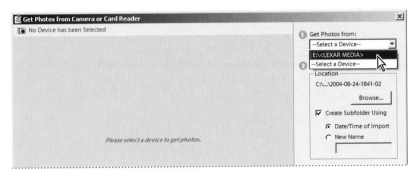

3 When the downloader finishes collecting thumbnails from the camera or memory card, scroll down the left side of the dialog box to see the thumbnails. Click the check boxes to deselect any images you don't want to download.

Drag the slider in the lower right corner of the thumbnails area to reduce or enlarge the size of the thumbnails. Or, click the icons at either end of the slider to jump to maximum or minimum thumbnail size.

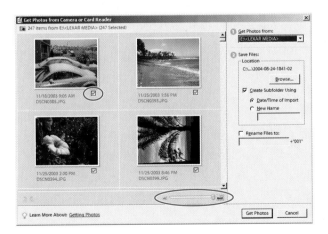

4 (Optional) On the right side of the Get Photos From Camera Or Card Reader dialog box, under (2) Save Files, select the options you want for storing the images:

• Leave Create Subfolder Using selected, which will store the downloaded images in a separate folder within the Digital Camera Photos folder.

• Either leave Date/Time Of Import selected (to name the folder something like 2004-08-24-1813-26 for August 24, 2004 at 4:13:26 PM), or select New Name and type a name in the space provided.

• Click Browse to see where the images will be stored. If you prefer a different location (the default is My Documents\My Pictures\Adobe\Digital Camera Photos), select it in the Browse For Folder dialog box, and click OK.

5 (Optional) Select Rename Files To, and type an appropriate prefix for the file name, such as 2004 Vacation to name the images 2004 Vacation001, 2004 Vacation002, 2004 Vacation003, and so forth.

6 Click Get Photos.

Photoshop Elements will go to work, downloading the images from the camera or memory card. When it finishes, the pictures will appear in Organizer.

Importing from a scanner

This exercise is also optional and requires that you have an available scanner. You can either do this procedure now or wait until later, when you're ready to start doing your own projects in Photoshop Elements 3.0.

1 Turn on your scanner, if it is not already on, and place the picture or document you want to scan in the scanner bed.

2 If the Get Photos From Scanner dialog box does not appear automatically, go to Photoshop Elements 3.0 Organizer and choose File > Get Photos > From Scanner.

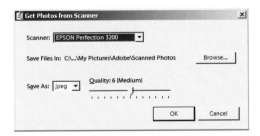

3 In the dialog box, do the following:

• Make sure that the correct scanner is selected in the Scanner pop-up menu (if you have more than one scanner installed).

• If you want to change the location in which the scanned files will be saved, choose Browse. Then find and select the folder you want to use.

• Either leave the default Save As settings unchanged, (JPEG) and Quality (6 Medium), or, if you are sure you want different settings, change them now.

• Click OK.

4 In the next dialog box, click Preview, and examine the resulting image.

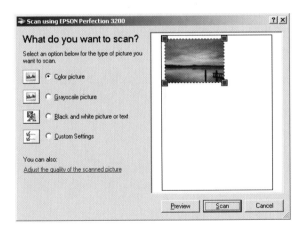

Note: The general appearance of the dialog box and the options available for your scanner may vary from those shown in the illustrations.

5 (Optional) If you want to make adjustments, click Adjust The Quality Of The Scanned Image, and change the settings in the Advanced Properties dialog box as needed. Then click OK.

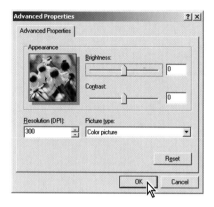

6 Click Scan.

When the scan is complete, the thumbnail appears in Organizer.

7 Click Back To All Images to see your entire catalog.

When you scan several photographs together, Photoshop Elements can automatically crop the scan into individual photos and straighten them. For more information on the Divide Scanned Photos feature, see Photoshop Elements Help.

Editing photos in Organizer

For complex editing, you'll want to use Photoshop Elements Editor, which you'll do in later lessons. But you can fix many common problems without leaving Organizer.

Rotating images

Sometimes you turn your camera sideways to take a photograph. That doesn't mean that you'll always have to look at a sideways image when the picture is on your computer.

1 Select the thumbnail of the tropical sunset, which is sideways.

2 Choose Edit > Rotate 90° Right, or hold down Ctrl and press the right arrow key.

Automatically fixing problems

Often a click or two is all it takes to bring out the best in your photographs.

1 Select the image of the Ferris wheel, which is dull in color.

2 Double-click the thumbnail, or drag the slider below it to the right to enlarge the view.

3 Choose Edit > Auto Smart Fix.

4 Choose Edit > Version Set > Reveal Photos In Version Set.

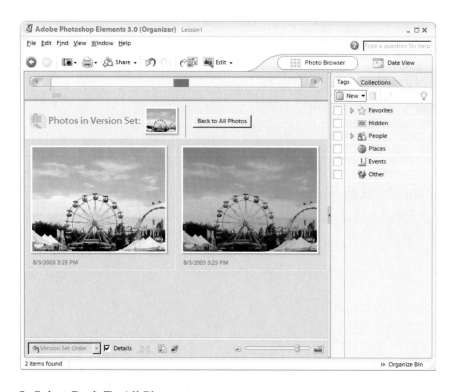

5 Select Back To All Photos.

Of course, there are many more sophisticated ways to fix photographs manually—but that's what other lessons in this book address.

Cropping photos

Cropping is the process of cutting out part of the photograph so that the composition focuses on the part of the image that you want to emphasize.

1 Select the image of the box of fishing flies.

2 Choose Edit > Auto Fix Window (being careful *not* to select Auto Smart Fix by mistake).

3 Select the Crop button. Then, under Aspect Ratio, select 3 x 4 (Portrait).

4 Drag the handles in the corners of the crop marquee so that only a small amount of blue tarp is visible around the box of fishing flies.

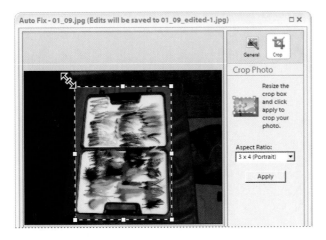

5 When you are satisfied with the proposed cropping area, click Apply. Then click OK to close the Auto Fix window.

6 When a message appears, telling you that the cropped version of the file has been saved under a different name, click OK.

Just as with the Auto Fix of the ferris wheel picture, the cropped and original images of the fishing flies are saved and appear together in a version set, as indicated by the icon () on the thumbnail. If you want to see the contents of the version set, use the same steps you used in the last part of the previous procedure.

Changing the date information

The image you'll work with in this procedure is a scan made in 2004 of a photograph taken many years earlier. The computer dates the image according to the date on which the file was created, which is the date of the scan.

You can instruct Photoshop Elements 3.0 Organizer to redate the image, so that it reflects the date of the event being pictured.

1 Find the photo of the two women in distinctive costumes, and click the date under the thumbnail. (Or, select the thumbnail and choose Edit > Adjust Date And Time.)

Note: If you do not see the date, look at the bottom of the Organizer window and make sure that the Details option is checked.

2 In the Adjust Date And Time dialog box, select Change To A Specified Date And Time, and click OK.

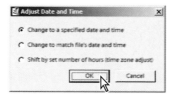

3 In the Set Date And Time dialog box, type **1985** under Year, and select December and 2 as the Month and Day.

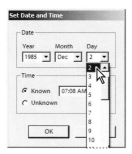

4 Under Time, do the following:

• Select Known.

• Select the hour and type **10**; then select the minutes and type **15**. (Or, select the time or hour and use the up and down arrow keys to change the time.)

• Click OK.

Now the picture of the two women appears as the last image in the thumbnail area.

E-mailing photos

Have you ever had to wait for minutes on end for an incoming e-mail to download, only to find that the problem was a single photograph that was huge in both file size and dimensions on the screen? Don't do that to your own friends and family!

You can avoid this inconvenience by using the Organizer e-mail function, which creates an optimized version of the image. Your e-mail buddies still get a clear, attractive photograph in an easily viewable size, but they don't have to wait for an enormous download.

1 Select the thumbnail of the tourists looking at the river gorge.

2 On the shortcuts bar, click Share ( ) and choose E-mail.

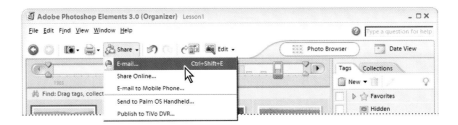

Note: If you haven't used e-mail on your computer before, a dialog box appears in which you can select a preferred e-mail application and enter your user name and e-mail address. After you click OK, the dialog box needed for Step 3 appears.

3 In the Attach Selected Items To E-mail dialog box, click Add Recipient.

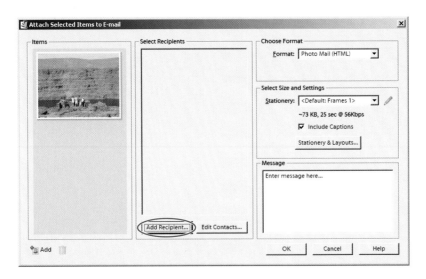

4 In the Add A Recipient dialog box, type in the first and last names (or a nickname—the example uses *Mom*) of the person to whom you want to send the picture, and the person's e-mail address. Leave the Add To Contact Book option selected, and click OK.

5 Back in the large Attach Selected Items to E-mail dialog box under Choose Format, select Individual Attachments from the pop-up menu.

6 Under Select Size And Quality, select Small (320 x 240).

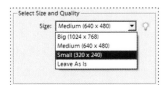

This reduces the file size from around 80 KB to about 36 KB. It also reduces the download time from 30 seconds to 12 seconds (for a typical 56 Kbps dial-up modem).

7 Under Message, delete the "Enter message here..." text, and type a message of your own, such as the one shown in the illustration. Then click OK.

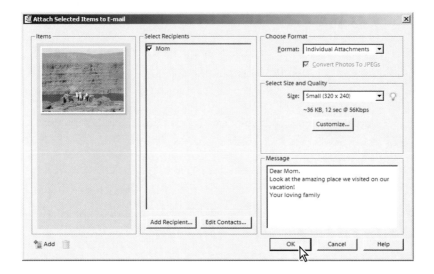

Your default e-mail application immediately creates an e-mail message. You can edit the message and Subject line as much as you want. When you are finished and ready to send the e-mail (make sure that you are connected to the Internet), either click Send (if you want to send an actual e-mail) or close the message without either saving or sending it.

Printing

Photoshop Elements 3.0 Organizer helps you reduce waste of expensive photographic paper. You can print single or multiple images on the same page, arranging them on the paper in the sizes you want.

1 Choose Edit > Select All to select all the thumbnails. Or, click one thumbnail to select it, and then hold down Ctrl and click several others.

2 Choose File > Print.

3 In the Print Selected Photos dialog box, make the following adjustments:

• Select an available printer.

• Under Select Type of Print, leave Individual Prints selected.

• Under Select Print Size And Options, select 3.5" x 5".

If a warning appears about print resolution, click OK to close it.

• Click the One Photo Per Page option to deselect it (remove the check mark).

4 (Optional) Do any of the following:

- On the left side of the dialog box, select one of the thumbnails and then click Remove (🗑) at the bottom of the thumbnails column to remove that image from the set that will be printed.

- Click Add (📷) under the column of thumbnails. Select Entire Catalog, and select the check box of any image thumbnail that you want to add to the set to be printed. Click OK.

- Under the Print Preview in the middle of the dialog box, click the arrows to see the other three pages that will be printed.

Note: You can select only images that are part of the current catalog. If you want to add other pictures to the printing batch, you must first add them to the catalog, using one of the methods you tried earlier in this lesson.

5 Do one of the following:

- Click Cancel to close the dialog box without printing. (This is recommended if you want to save your color ink and photograph paper for your own images.)

- Click Print to actually print the pictures.

Viewing photo thumbnails

There are various ways of viewing your Organizer catalog. Some of the options are merely matters of your preferred work flow or work habits. Others actually enable a number of efficiencies that can speed up your work with photographs.

Using Photo Browser view

Up to this point, you've been working in the default Photo Browser view. There are a few other options that you should be aware of.

1 In the pop-up menu in the lower left corner of the Organizer window, select Import Batch to see the thumbnails organized by their separate import sessions.

Notice the bar separating the rows of thumbnails, with the film canister icon.

2 Try the following:

• Click the separator bar between batches (reading "Imported from hard disk on...") to select the thumbnails of all images imported in that session.

• Enlarge the thumbnail size by dragging the slider below the thumbnail area.

• Click one of the three bars in the graph above the thumbnails area to jump to the first image imported in that session.

The view switches to the first image in that batch, the date for that image flashes off and on, and a green border temporarily surrounds the image.

3 Reduce the thumbnail size again before you continue, making it small enough so that you can see all the images in your catalog.

4 Using the same pop-up menu that you used in Step 1, select Folder Location to see the thumbnails organized according to the folders in which they are stored on your computer. Then try the same two experiments that you did in Step 2.

5 Using the same pop-up menu, select Date (Newest First). Select one of the bars in the graph above the thumbnails to jump to the photograph taken at that point in the time line.

Using Date View

If you are working with a collection of pictures that spans a number of years, you are going to appreciate Date View.

1 Select Date View (▦) on the right end of the shortcuts bar.

2 Select the Year option under the calendar display, if it is not already selected. Use the forward and back arrows on either side of the year heading in the calendar to go to 2004, if it is not already selected.

3 Select March 25 on the 2004 calendar.

A preview of the photograph taken on March 25 appears on the right.

4 Select the Month option under the calendar display, and then select March 6 on the calendar, where there's already a thumbnail of a flower photograph.

5 Under the flower thumbnail on the right, click the Next Item On Selected Day arrow to see a second photograph taken on the same date.

6 Using the date at the top of the calendar, do the following:

• Click the word *March* and choose August from the pop-up menu that appears.

• Click 2004 in the calendar heading and choose 2003 from the pop-up menu.

7 Click in the Daily Note area and type **County Fair** to add a note to the date.

Now that you know how to change the date to review your images, you can reset Organizer to your preferred settings whenever you want to do so. For these lessons, you'll need to go back to Photo Browser rather than Date View.

Organizing photos

Most of us find it challenging to organize our files and folders efficiently. It's easy to forget which pictures were stored in what folder. It's tedious to have to open and examine the contents of numerous folders, looking for the needed image or file.

The good news is that such searches are a thing of the past. You saw earlier how you can use the Search feature in Organizer to find and import files from multiple locations on your computer. The next set of topics will show you how a little time invested in tags can streamline the process of sorting through your pictures, regardless of where the actual image files might be stored.

Applying tags to photos

Tags and tag categories are search criteria—like keywords, if you're familiar with that term—that you apply to images. In this example, you'll apply a couple of tags from the default set to one of the images you imported into your catalog.

1 In the shortcuts bar, click Photo Browser ( ), and make sure that Date (Newest First) is selected in the lower left corner of the Organizer window.

2 In the Tags palette, select the Places category tag, and drag it to the first thumbnail, which shows people looking over a river gorge.

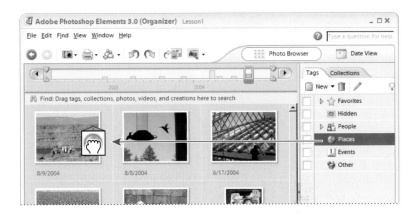

3 Click the arrow next to the People category to expand it so that you can see the Family and Friends sub-categories.

4 Drag the Family subcategory tag to the same thumbnail (the people by the river gorge).

5 Allow the pointer to rest for a few seconds over the tags below the river-gorge thumbnail until a tool tip appears, identifying the tags that are applied to the image.

Creating new categories and sub-categories

The default set of tags is limited. You can add or delete new categories and sub-categories to suit your own projects.

1 In the Tags palette, click New to open a pop-up menu, and choose New Category.

2 In the Create Category dialog box, type **Animals**, and select the bird symbol under Category Icon. Click OK.

3 In the Tags palette, select the People category. Then click New at the top of the palette, and choose New Sub-Category.

4 In the Create Sub-Category dialog box, type **Strangers**. Make sure that People is shown in the Parent Category Or Sub-Category option, and click OK.

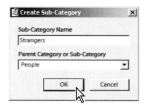

The new tag categories become part of this catalog. They will not appear in any new catalogs that you create, but there are ways to work around that, too. (See Photoshop Elements 3.0 Help for more information.)

Applying and editing category assignments

You can add tags to several files at once, and you can also delete tags from an image.

1 In the thumbnails, select the picture of the hummingbirds, and then hold down Ctrl and click the seagull picture to select it, too.

2 Drag the Animals tag to either one of the two selected bird thumbnails to apply the tag to both pictures.

3 Drag the Strangers sub-category to the river-gorge image. (It is not necessary to select the thumbnail or to deselect the other two thumbnails.)

4 Select the river-gorge thumbnail, and open the Properties palette by doing one of the following:

• Choose Window > Properties.

• Below the thumbnails area, click the Show Or Hide Properties ( ) icon.

5 Select Tags ( ) in the Properties palette to see which tags are applied to this image.

6 Remove the Family tag from the river-gorge image by doing one of the following:

• Right-click the People tag below it and choose Remove Family Sub-Category Tag.

• In the Properties palette, right-click the Family, Strangers listing and choose Remove Family Sub-Category Tag.

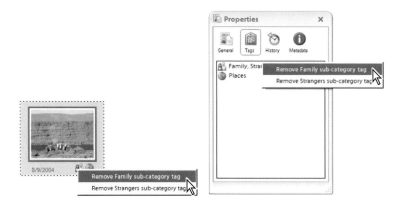

7 Close the Properties palette by clicking Close (✕) in the upper right corner or by clicking Show Or Hide Properties (▣) again.

Creating and applying new tags

In the previous topic, you created new tag categories and subcategories. In this topic, you'll create a new tag, which must be added under a specific category or subcategory.

1 In the Tags palette, do the following:

• Select the Other category.

• Click New, and choose New Tag.

2 In the Create Tag dialog box, type **Architecture** for Name, and click OK.

3 Drag the Architecture tag to the ornate Victorian building (taken April 8, 2003).

The image of the building becomes the tag icon because it's the first image to get this tag.

4 Drag the Architecture tag to the ferris wheel and the multi-angled glass interior, so that three images have that tag.

Note: You can also use the Collections tab of the Organizer Bin to define collections of images within a catalog. Collections have some similarities to tags and some unique features and limitations. For more information, see Photoshop Elements 3.0 Help.

Converting tags and categories

It's easy to change the hierarchy of categories and tags, promoting or demoting them whenever you like. Doing this does not remove the tags or categories from the images to which you've assigned them.

1 In the Tags palette, drag the Animals category to the Other category.

Now the Animals category appears as a sub-category under Other. Because it's no longer a category, it has the generic sub-category icon instead of the bird icon.

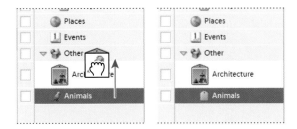

2 Under the People category, right-click the Strangers sub-category, and choose Change Strangers Sub-category To A Tag.

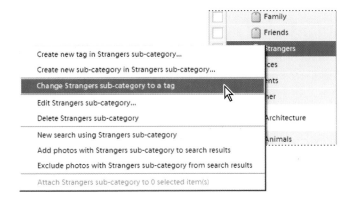

3 In the Tabs palette, select the Strangers tag, and click Edit ( ) at the top of the Tags palette.

4 In the Edit Tag dialog box, click Edit Icon to open the Edit Tag Icon dialog box.

5 Drag the corners of the boundary in the thumbnail so that it just surrounds the group of people in the image.

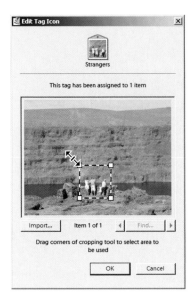

6 Click OK to close the dialog box and again to close the Edit Tag dialog box.

💡 *When you have tagged several images with the same tag, as you've done with the Architecture tag, you can select a different picture for the tag icon. Do this in the Edit Tag Icon dialog box, using the Find button or its arrows to select a different image.*

Applying more tags to images

There are a few simple ways to automatically tag multiple images, as well as manual methods you can use for custom tags.

1 In the view pop-up menu in the lower left corner of the Organizer window, choose Folder Location.

2 Click Instant Tag on the right end of the separator bar above the first set of thumbnails.

3 In the Create And Apply New Tag dialog box, choose Other in the Category pop-up menu, leaving Batch1 for Name, and then click OK.

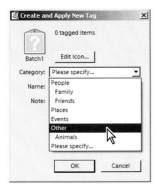

4 Repeat Steps 2 and 3 for the other two (or more) folder groups, Batch2 and Batch3.

5 Switch back to Date (Newest First) view, using the same menu you used in Step 1.

6 Apply the Strangers tags to any image picturing a person you don't know.

7 (Optional) Create and apply any other tags or categories you might want. For example, you could create a Flowers or Fishing tag, category, or sub-category.

Using tags to find pictures

Why create all these tags? Because they make it amazingly simple to find your pictures.

1 Click the empty Find box next to the Architecture tag.

A binoculars icon appears in the Find box to remind you that it is selected. Now only the three thumbnails tagged with Architecture appear.

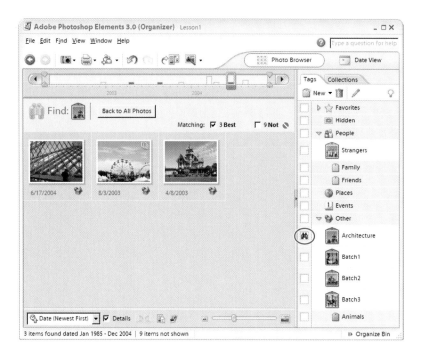

2 Leave the Architecture tag selected, and click the Find box for the Batch2 tag.

Now only two thumbnails appear: the two that are tagged both for Architecture and for Batch2.

3 In the Matching check boxes above the thumbnails, select Not and then click Best to deselect it.

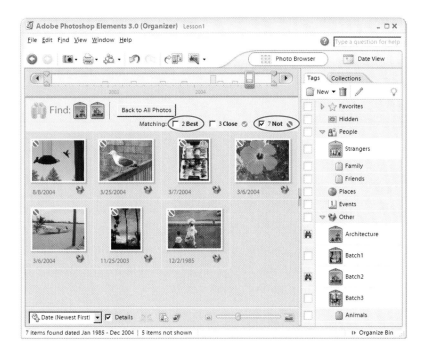

The thumbnails display changes, showing only images that are not tagged for either Architecture or Batch2.

4 Click Back To All Photos.

You'll use tags many times in the process of completing other lessons in this book.

Congratulations! You've just finished your first lesson, and we're hoping that you feel pretty good about your accomplishment.

In this lesson, you've imported files into Photoshop Elements 3.0 Organizer, using various techniques. You've used several handy tools for quickly completing basic editing tasks, such as rotating images, cropping, and applying an automatic fixing feature. You have seen how you can share images by e-mail without creating huge download delays for your addressees, and how to set up single or multiple images for printing. Finally, you've created, edited, and applied tags to individual photographs so that they'll be easy to find in future work sessions.

Review questions

1 How do you open the Organizer component of Adobe Photoshop Elements 3.0?

2 What's the best and fastest way to add all the images on your computer to your Organizer catalog, regardless of where they are located in your folder structure?

3 Name several ways you can make it easier to find specific photos in your catalog.

4 Where is the shortcuts bar?

5 How do you print multiple images on a single sheet of paper?

6 Why should you use Organizer to prepare photos for e-mail?

Review answers

1 There are several ways to open the Organizer. You can select View And Organize Photos on the Welcome screen when you start Photoshop Elements 3.0. Or, if Photoshop Elements Editor is already open, you can select Photo Browser at the top of the work area. If you always want to open Photoshop Elements in Organizer, use the Start Up In pop-up menu in the lower left border of the Welcome screen to choose Organizer.

2 The most effortless way to catalog all your images is to choose File > Get Photos > By Searching, and then selecting your hard disk for Look In. This method collects all images, regardless of how disorganized they might be in your folders.

3 You can find photos by file location, by date, by import batch, and by using tags. The pop-up menu in the lower left corner of Organizer determines the order in which the thumbnails appear, such as Date (Newest First) or File Location. For a calendar view of your images, click Date View ( ) on the shortcuts bar. You can also use the Find menu, which offers many more ways to set search criteria. Select Find boxes for a tag to limit the thumbnail display to images with that tag.

4 The shortcuts bar is just below the menus (File, Edit, and so on).

5 All multi-photo printing with Photoshop Elements is done in Organizer, although you can start the process in Editor, too. You start by selecting the photo or photos you want to print, and choosing File > Print. Then deselect One Photos Per Page.

6 The Organizer feature for attaching photos to e-mail creates and attaches versions of your photos that are appropriate for e-mail. This means it's faster to send them, faster for others to download them, and people will be able to see them without scrolling.

2 | Learning by Playing with Text

Crisp, flexible, and editable text fits neatly into your Photoshop Elements 3.0 workflow. Whether you need straightforward, classic typography or wild effects and wacky colors, it's all possible.

This lesson is about much more than text, but using text is a good way to introduce yourself to editing photographs with Photoshop Elements 3.0. Even if you think you'll rarely use text in your work, you're encouraged to do this lesson first, before you go on to correcting images and working creatively with other features.

In this lesson, you'll learn how to do the following:

- Use prepared Organizer tags to locate the start files for the five projects.

- Add a border to an image by changing the canvas size.

- Select a tool and change its settings in the tool options bar.

- Format, add, and edit text, including adding special effects and warping it.

- Apply Effects and Layer Styles to text.

- Move image layers independently.

- Hide and reveal layers.

- Transfer a layer from one image to another.

- Add a Shape layer.

- Merge two layers into a single layer.

- Create a simple animation.

- Optimize images for maximum efficiency.

Before you begin, make sure that you've correctly copied the project files from the *Adobe Photoshop Elements 3.0 Classroom in a Book* CD (attached to the inside of the back cover of this book). See "Copying the Classroom in a Book files" on page 3.

This lesson is a long one, with five relatively lengthy projects. Each project builds on the skills learned in the ones before it. Most people need about half an hour to complete each of the five projects, so you might plan to do the lesson in more than one work session.

This lesson assumes that you are already familiar with general features of the Photoshop Elements 3.0 work area and that you recognize the two ways in which you can use Photoshop Elements: Editor and Organizer. You are welcome to go ahead and start with this chapter, even if you haven't done Lesson 1, but most users should do all the lessons in the order presented. If you discover that you need more background information as you proceed, see Photoshop Elements Help, the Tutorials available on the Welcome screen, or the *Adobe Photoshop Elements 3.0 Getting Started Guide*.

Getting started

In Lesson 1, you worked exclusively with the Organizer component of Photoshop Elements 3.0. Lesson 2 introduces you to the Editor component of the application. Using Editor, you can build layers to bring photos together with text and other elements.

In this lesson, you'll use the catalog you copied from the CD and reconnected to its image files in the Getting Started chapter (see "Copying the Classroom in a Book files" on page 3) instead of the one you created in Lesson 1.

1 Start Photoshop Elements. On the Welcome screen, select View And Organize Photos.

2 Choose File > Catalog.

3 In the Catalog dialog box, click Open.

4 In the Open Catalog dialog box, select the CIB catalog.psa file (or, if you renamed the file in the Getting Started chapter, select that file), and click Open.

If you do not see the CIB catalog file, review the procedures you did in the Getting Started chapter, or do those procedures now. See "Copying the Lessons files from the CD" on page 3, and "Reconnecting missing files to a catalog" on page 6.

Project 1: Placing a text label on an image

This project will involve typing, formatting, and arranging text on an existing photograph. The goal is to make an image look like a print from an instant camera, and then to add a label on the border of the print. You might use the completed image file in the layout of a web page, presentation, or electronic scrapbook.

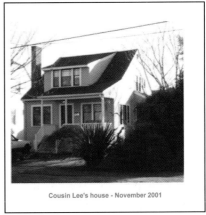

Cousin Lee's house - November 2001

Using Organizer to find and open tagged files

1 If Photoshop Elements is not already open in Organizer, open it now, following the procedure above in "Getting started" on page 51.

2 Make sure that the Organize Bin is open, so that you can see the list of Tags. Or, open it now by clicking the Organize Bin arrow (▮▶) in the lower right corner of the work area.

3 In the Tags palette, click once on the word Imported Tags to select it. Click the Pencil icon at the top of the palette to edit this category. When the Edit Category window opens enter the Category Name **Lessons** for this category, replacing the Imported Tags Category Name. Click OK. You can rename categories after they have been created by using this process.

4 At the top of the Tags palette, click the New drop-down menu and choose New Category. Enter the Category Name **Projects** and choose an icon for this category. We selected the gear icon available at the far right of the scrolling window. Click OK after entering the name and selecting an icon. You will now add several images to the Projects category.

5 If necessary, expand the Lessons category by clicking the small arrow to the left of the word Lessons. Hold down the Ctrl key on your keyboard and click once on each of the Project tags in the Tags palette to select the all of them. You should have the individual tags labeled Project 1 through Project 7 selected, but not the Projects category. If the Projects category is selected, Ctrl-click on it to deselect it.

6 While the Projects tags are selected, click on any one of the selected tags and drag it on top of the category labeled Projects. All of the project tags should now be organized under the Projects category.

7 Click the Lesson 2 tag Find box, located to the left of the name Lesson 2 in the Tags palette.

Now the thumbnails show only the seven image files that you'll use in this lesson.

8 Expand the Projects tag, and click the Project 1 Find box.

Only one image is tagged with both the Lesson 2 and Project 1 tags, so only one thumbnail appears.

9 Select the thumbnail and then click Edit (🖼️) in the shortcuts bar (*not* the Edit menu in the menu bar), and choose Go To Standard Edit.

Note: If an error message appears saying that the file is missing, that means that the link to the image file has been broken. See "Reconnecting missing files to a catalog" on page 6.

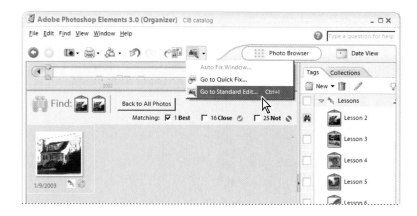

Adding an uneven border

In this procedure, you'll enlarge the *canvas*—the area on which the image appears—without increasing the size of the *image*. The canvas size is usually the same as the image size for digital photographs, but you can enlarge it to add a border. The border area takes on the color currently selected as the Background Color, which is comparable to the paper underlying a photographic print.

In this procedure, you'll create this border in two phases and give it precise dimensions.

1 In Photoshop Elements 3.0 Editor and with the 02_01.jpg file open, choose Image > Resize > Canvas Size.

2 In the Canvas Size dialog box, do the following in the same order as they are listed:

• Select the Relative check box.

• In Width, type **0.5** and select Inches from the pop-up menu.

- In Height, type **0.5** and select Inches from the pop-up menu.

- Select the center square in the Anchor diagram.

- Select White for the Canvas Extension Color.

- Click OK to close the dialog box and apply the changes. A uniformly sized white border now surrounds the image.

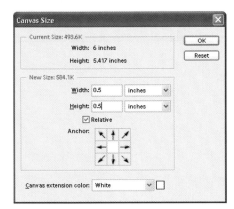 

3 Choose Image > Resize > Canvas Size again, and enter the following options:

- In the Anchor diagram, select the center square in the top row.

- In Height, type **0.75**. (Make sure Width is 0, or enter that now.)

- Leave all other settings unchanged, and click OK.

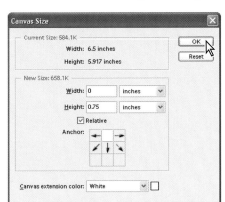 

Now the border has grown taller but only in the area under the image.

Adding a quick border

When precision isn't important for the canvas-size enlargement, you can use the Crop tool to do the job.

1. *Select the Zoom tool ( ) and zoom out by holding down Alt (the pointer will change from a magnifying glass with a plus sign ( ) to one with a minus sign ( ) and clicking. If necessary, click again until you can see some of the gray pasteboard surrounding the image.*

2. *Select the Crop tool ( ) and drag a rectangle within the image—size doesn't matter at this point.*

3. *Drag the corner handles of the crop marquee outside of the image area onto the pasteboard to define the size and shape of border that you want to create.*

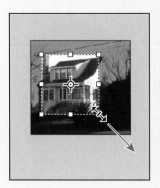  

4. *Click Commit ( ) on the tool options bar to apply the change. Or, click Cancel ( ) next to the Commit icon if you don't want to crop the image.*

The Background Color (the default is White) fills in the added area of the canvas.

Formatting and typing a text layer

You set up the formatting—font family, font size, text color, and so forth—in the tool options bar. The settings available in the tool options bar change according to what tool is active. The options for text formatting appear only after you select the Type tool, so that's your first step.

1   In the toolbox, select the Horizontal Type tool (T).

2   In the tool options bar, select the following from the pop-up menus:

• For font family, select Arial or another sans-serif font.

• For font style, select Bold, if it is available for the selected font family.

• For font size, select 14 pt.

3 Click anywhere on the lower left side of the image window to set the cursor, and type **Cousin Lee's house - November 1989**

Note: Don't worry about any typing errors you might make or the exact position of the text in the image, because you'll correct those things a little later.

4 Click Commit (✔) in the tool options bar to accept the text. Or, press Enter on the numeric keypad.

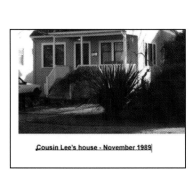
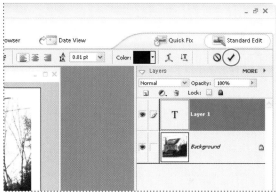

Note: Do not press the Enter key on the central part of your keyboard to accept text changes. When the Type tool is active, that key creates a line break in the text instead of committing the changes.

5 Select the Move tool (▸⊕) in the toolbox.

6 Place the pointer inside the text so that the pointer turns into a solid black arrowhead (▸) and drag it so that the text is more or less centered on the lower border of the image.

In the Palette Bin on the right side of the work area, the Layers palette shows that the image is now made up of two layers, a Background and a text layer above it. Most of the text layer is transparent, so only the text itself blocks your view of the Background layer. (If the Layers palette isn't in the Palette Bin, choose Window > Layers to open it. Also see the sidebar, "Using the Palette Bin" on the next page.)

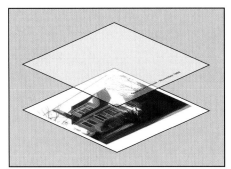

Diagram of the layer structure, and Layers palette

Note: *There are other tools for typing text besides the Horizontal Type tool. In the rest of this book, the term* Type tool *always refers to the Horizontal Type tool, which is the default type tool.*

Using the Palette Bin

By default, the How To, Styles And Effects, and Layers palettes are in the Palette Bin. Other palettes you open (using the Window menu) float in the work area. You can change which palettes float and which are stored in the Palette Bin.

To remove palettes from the Palette Bin and close them

1. *Drag the title bar out of the Palette Bin.*

2. *Click the More button on the palette to open the palette menu, and deselect Place In Palette Bin.*

3. *Click Close (✕) on the palette title bar, or choose Window > [palette name] to close it.*

To add floating palettes to the Palette Bin

1. *Choose Window > [palette name] to open the palette you want to place in the Palette Bin.*

2. *Drag the palette by its tab (the name itself, not by the colored bar above the name) to the Palette Bin.*

The Place In Palette Bin command does not move a palette into the Palette Bin. This command affects what happens when you click the Close button of a floating palette. When Place In Palette Bin is selected, clicking the Close button restores the palette to the Palette Bin rather than closing it.

To adjust palette sizes in the Palette Bin

Adjust the height of palettes by doing either or both of the following:

- *Click the arrow on the left side of palette title bars to minimize or expand them as needed.*

- *Drag the separator bars between palettes up or down to enlarge or reduce the height of the palettes.*

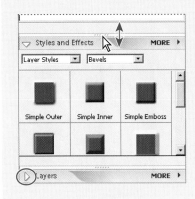

Editing a text layer

Adding text is a nondestructive process, so your original image is not overwritten by the text. Even after you save and close your work file, you can reopen it and move, edit, or delete the text layer without hurting the image at all.

Using the Type tool works much like typing in a word-processing application. If you want to change attributes (such as font, color, and so forth), you select the characters you want to change, and then adjust the settings.

1 If necessary, choose View > Zoom In to enlarge the image until you can comfortably read the text.

2 Make sure that the text layer (Cousin Lee's house) is selected in the Layers palette and that the Type tool (T) is selected.

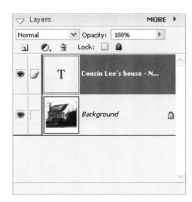

3 Double-click the date, 1989, to select it, and type **2001**.

4 Move the cursor to the beginning of the text and drag to the end to select it all.

5 In the tool options bar, click the arrow beside the Color option and select a swatch of another color, such as blue or red, that will stand out against the white image border.

Note: If you accidentally click the Color sample in the tool options bar instead of the little arrow, you'll open the Color Picker, which is a different way to select colors, but not quite as intuitive as the Samples palette.)

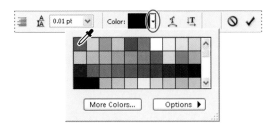

6 Correct any typing errors you may have made:

• Click once to move the insertion point to another position within the text, or use the arrow keys to move the cursor forward or back.

• Click and drag to select multiple characters.

• Type to add text or to overwrite selected characters.

• Press Backspace or Delete to erase characters.

7 Select Commit (✓) in the tool options bar to accept your editing changes.

Saving a work file

In this procedure, you'll set up a special folder for your work files. You'll use this folder as the location for your results for all projects in this book.

1 Choose File > Save.

2 Using the Save In pop-up menu, navigate to the Lessons folder (one level up from the Lessons 2 folder). Click the Create New Folder button. Type **My CIB Work** in the File Name area, and then click Open.

Note: CIB *stands for* Classroom in a Book.

3 In File Name, type **02_01_Work**.

4 In Format, make sure that Photoshop (PSD) is selected.

5 Under Save Options, make sure that Include In Organizer is selected. Then deselect Save In Version Set With Original.

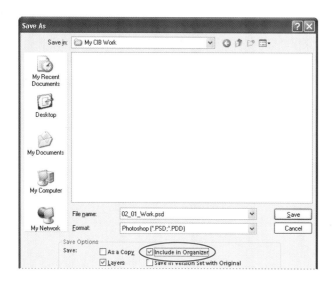

6 Review your settings to be sure that they match the illustration above, and click Save.

7 Choose File > Close. When a message appears, click No to close the original file in its unchanged condition.

If a message appears about Format Options, click OK to close it.

Note: If you want to prevent the message from appearing in the future, use the Edit menu (Edit > Preferences > Saving Files) after you close the message to open the Preferences dialog box. In the Maximize PSD File Compatibility pop-up menu, choose either Always or Never, and then click OK. In either case, the message will not reappear each time you save a file in PSD format.

Version Sets and automatic renaming of edited files are workflow conveniences introduced in Photoshop Elements 3.0. For purposes of this book, you won't use them, but you should look into these features later, for your personal projects. See Photoshop Elements 3.0 Help for more information.

Congratulations, you've finished your first text project. In this section, you've done much more than just type a few words. You've formatted and edited the text. You've seen how layers work independently in an image. You've enlarged the canvas size without stretching the image itself. If you're ready to go on, close this work file (File > Close).

Project 2: Making cartoon balloons

In Project One for this lesson, you saw how the text floated above the original photograph on its own layer. In this project, you'll go one step farther and add an intermediate layer.

Your goal is one you've probably seen on humorous greeting cards, where the artist has combined a cartoon speech balloon with a photograph to put words in the mouth of the person or animal pictured. It's a fun thing to do with group photographs, to tell a story in a lighthearted way.

Opening the image file for Project 2

You'll start by finding and opening the file, using Organizer tags.

1 If Photoshop Elements is open in Editor mode, click Photo Browser ( ) on the shortcuts bar to switch to Organizer.

2 If the Back To All Photos button appears above the thumbnails, select it now.

3 On the Tags tab, click the Find boxes for the Lesson 2 and Project 2 tags so that the only thumbnail with both these tags appears.

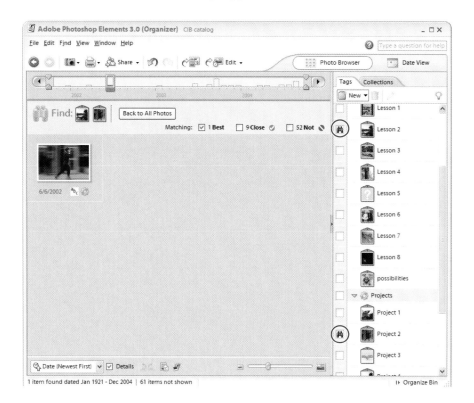

4 Select the image thumbnail.

5 Click Edit (⬛) on the shortcuts bar, and choose Go To Standard Edit.

Drawing a cartoon balloon in one stroke

In this procedure, you'll use a couple of items that appear when you click or hold down the mouse over a specific part of the work area. The first type is a list of tools grouped with another tool in the toolbox. The second is a palette menu. Palette menus are available for some palettes, but not all. They provide additional commands and choices that apply to items shown in the palette.

1 In the toolbox, press the Rectangle tool (▣) until a list appears showing all the shape tools. Select the Custom Shape tool (◔).

Note: *Be careful not to confuse the Gradient tool (▬) or Rectangular Marquee tool (▢) for the Rectangle tool.*

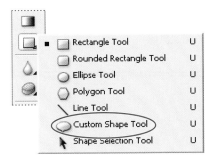

Notice that the Custom Shape-tool icon replaces the Rectangle-tool icon in the toolbox.

2 In the tool options bar, click the Shape arrow to open the pop-up palette of custom shapes. Then click the small arrow (▸) to open the palette menu, and choose Talk Bubbles.

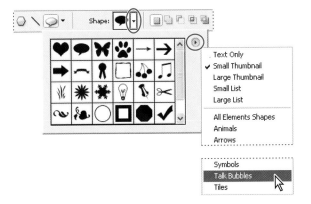

3 Select your choice of Talk Bubble shapes, and press Enter to close the palette.

(The example uses the Talk 10 shape, but you can try any Talk Bubble shape.)

4 Drag diagonally to draw a balloon beside the man.

5 Click the arrow by the Color swatch in the tool options bar, and select a swatch from the palette. Or, you can skip this step and leave the color unchanged.

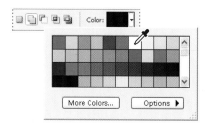

6 Select the Move tool (⊹) and do the following, as needed:

• To move the balloon, move the pointer inside the shape and drag.

• To resize the shape, drag the corners of the shape bounding box.

7 If the Commit icon (✔) appears on the tool options bar, click it, or press Enter.

Note: If you resize the shape, the Commit step is required. If you only move the shape, the Commit and Cancel buttons do not appear.

A quick glance at the Layers palette shows you that the Custom Shape tool automatically created a new layer, Shape 1.

Adding text over the custom shape

In this procedure, you'll get a chance to practice the basic techniques for text that you used in Project 1 of this lesson. You'll discover one important difference between text layers you create in Photoshop Elements and text you type in a word-processing application. That difference has to do with line breaks. While many applications automatically wrap the text at the end of a line, you must manually enter line breaks in Photoshop Elements.

1 In the toolbox, select the Type tool (T).

2 In the tool options bar, select the following from the pop-up menus:

• For font family, select a sans serif font, such as Arial.

• For font style, select Bold.

• For font size, select **14** pt.

• For paragraph alignment, select Center Text (≡).

• For Color, make sure the swatch is black, or click the arrow to open the Color Swatches palette and select Black. Click anywhere outside the Color Swatches palette to close it.

3 Click to place a text insertion point near the upper center of the balloon shape, and then type a few words or some nonsense syllables, such as **Yakkity yakkity** or **Hello?**

4 Press Enter on the keyboard (*not* on the numeric keypad) to create a line break, and then type more words or nonsense syllables.

5 Using the same techniques you used in Project 1, edit the text as needed to correct any typing errors, and then click Commit (✔) in the tool options bar.

6 Using the Move tool (▸⊕), drag the text block to center it over the talk balloon shape.

💡 *When the Move tool is selected, you can use the arrow keys to nudge the layer in small increments instead of dragging it. Similarly, you can use the arrow keys to nudge a selection when a selection tool is active.*

7 Choose File > Save. In the Save As dialog box, name the file **02_02_Work**, and save it as a Photoshop (PSD) file in the My CIB Work folder that you created during the previous project. If Save In Version Set With Original is selected, be sure to deselect it before you click Save. (See "Saving a work file" on page 62.)

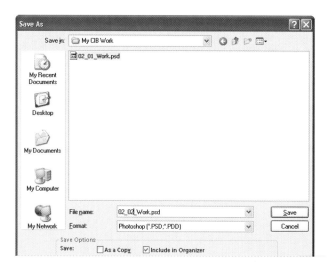

The file you've created now has three layers: the Background (the original photograph image), the Shape 1 layer, and the text layer. Each layer can be changed independently of the other two.

Congratulations, you've finished another project. In the process, you've gained experience creating custom shape layers, adding text, and editing text. Close this project work file (choose File > Close) without saving the changes to the original photo.

Project 3: Embossing text on an image

Thus far in Lesson 2, you've saved projects in a work file that preserves the layering. This gives you the maximum flexibility to go back later and make changes without having to rebuild the image from the beginning or damaging the original photos.

In this lesson, you'll do what professional photographic studios sometimes do to protect proprietary images. You will apply an embossing effect, so that it looks as if words have been pressed into a print of the images.

Creating a new document for the text

You'll start by preparing the text in its own file. In this procedure, you'll see a gray-and-white checkerboard pattern. This pattern indicates 100% transparency, where the area or layer acts like a pane of glass or a sheet of clear acetate on which you can add items.

1 In Photoshop Elements Editor, choose File > New > Blank File.

2 In the New dialog box, do all of the following:

- For Name, type **Emboss_text**.

- For Width, type **640** and select Pixels.

- For Height, type **425** and select Pixels.

- For Resolution, type **72** and select Pixels/inch.

- For Color Mode, select RGB Color.

- For Background Contents, select Transparent.

• Review your settings to make sure they are correct, and click OK.

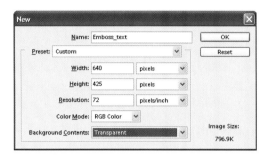

The image window shows only a checkerboard pattern. (If it does not, choose Edit > Undo, and repeat Step 2, being careful to select Transparent from the Background Contents pop-up menu.) The pattern symbolizes transparency.

3 Select the Type tool (T), and then use the tool options bar to set the text attributes with the font family (a sans serif font is best), the style as Bold, and the font size as 48 pt. Also select Left Align Text (≡).

4 Click near the left side of the image window and type **COPYRIGHT 2005** (or the current year). Click Commit (✔) in the tool options bar to accept the text you've typed.

5 Select the Move tool (▶⊕) and drag the text to center it in the image window.

6 Move the Move tool outside a corner of the text-layer bounding box, so that the pointer appears as a curved, double-ended arrow (↰), and drag left or right to rotate the text.

You can also resize or reshape the text by dragging corners of the bounding box so that it fits properly on the diagonal.

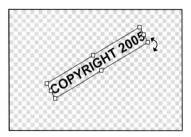 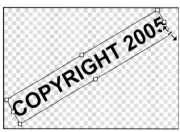

7 Click Commit (✔) on the tool options bar.

Photoshop Elements text layers are vector shapes, based on mathematics rather than pixels. Consequently, text and other vector shapes remain smooth even if you drag the corners of the bounding box to enlarge them. If you tried this with bitmap text, you'd see jagged, stair-step edges in the resized text.

Adding the text to multiple images

Now that you've prepared the text, you'll need some pictures in which to place it.

1 Click Photo Browser (⌘) on the shortcuts bar in the upper part of the work area to switch to Organizer. If the Back To All Photos button appears above the thumbnails, select it now.

2 On the Tags tab, click the Find boxes for the Lesson 2 and Project 3 tags to find the thumbnails for the three images you'll use for this project.

3 Choose Edit > Select All, and then click Edit (⌘) on the shortcuts bar, and choose Go To Standard Edit.

4 On the right side of the menu bar, click the Tile icon (⊞) to automatically resize and arrange the four open images in the work area. Or, choose Window > Images > Tile.

5 In the Photo Bin (the row of thumbnails across the bottom of the work area on the left), select the COPYRIGHT thumbnail to make it the active file.

6 In the Layers palette, hold down Shift and drag the layer thumbnail for the COPYRIGHT text layer and drop it in the center of the 02_03_a, the snow scene.

7 Repeat Step 6 for the 02_03_b.jpg and 02_03_c.jpg images, dragging the original COPYRIGHT text layer onto those images.

You can close the text file you created, Emboss_text.psd and save it in the My CIB Work folder.

💡 *You can change the zoom level of all open images at once. Select one image and choose View > Zoom In or View > Zoom Out until you reach the zoom level you want. Then choose Window > Images > Match Zoom. All the other open files will immediately zoom to the same percentage view as the selected file.*

Applying the embossing effect to the text layer

In this procedure, you'll try out an Effect—one of the specialty features in Photoshop Elements. Effects are complex combinations of adjustments that you apply in one easy action. Because these adjustments are art attributes instead of font attributes, the text layer must be *simplified* before you can apply the Effect.

1 In the Photo Bin, select the 02_03_a.jpg thumbnail (the winter scene), and then select the text layer in the Layers palette.

2 In the Palette Bin, click the arrow by the Styles And Effects palette to expand it, if necessary.

3 At the top of the Styles And Effects palette, select Effects and then Text Effects in the pop-up menus.

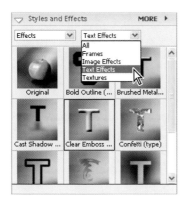

4 Double-click the Clear Emboss effect thumbnail to apply it to the selected text layer.

In the Layers palette, the COPYRIGHT layer thumbnail changes to one for an art layer, not a text layer.

5 Repeat Step 4 to apply the Clear Emboss effect to the text layers in the 02_03_b.jpg and then the 02_03_c.jpg files.

6 Choose Window > Images > Cascade to turn off Automatic Tile mode and to arrange the open image windows in one step.

Saving copies of the images for web use

Your final task for this project is to convert the files back to JPEG format. This reduces the file size, which makes it more efficient for web use. But the conversion also flattens each image file so that the words and the original image are merged into one inseparable layer.

In this topic, you'll use the Save For Web feature, using a large dialog box that covers the entire work area. In it, two views of the image file appear side by side. The left version shows you the original image with its original quality settings. The right version reflects the resolutions, format, size, and other settings you enter on the far right side of the dialog box, and shows you file size and other information below the image.

1 In the Photo Bin, select the 02_03_a thumbnail, and choose File > Save For Web.

2 Under the two views of the image, notice the file-size information. The Original view indicates that the file size of the PSD file is close to the megabyte range.

Note: You can use the Zoom tool (🔍*) in the upper left corner of the dialog box to zoom in or (by holding down Alt and clicking) zoom out. Use the Hand tool (*✋*) to drag both images at once, so that you see the same details in both views.*

3 On the right side of the dialog box, select JPEG High in the Preset pop-up menu.

Notice the change in the file size for the JPEG view of the image, which is about 60 KB.

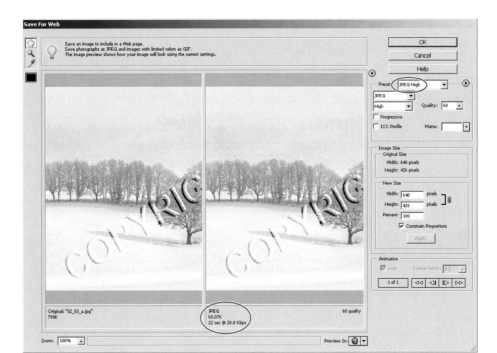

4 Under New Size, select Constrain Proportions, and type **480** in the Width option.

Because you selected Constrain Proportions, the Height automatically changes.

5 Click Apply (still in the New Size area of the dialog box), and then look at the file size under the JPEG view of the image.

Note: If you need to reduce the file size even more, you can select JPEG Medium or JPEG Low. You can select intermediate levels between these options by changing the Quality value, either by typing a different number or by clicking the arrow and dragging the slider.

6 Click OK, and select the My CIB Work folder as the location and **02_03_a_final** as the File Name in the Save Optimized As dialog box, and click Save.

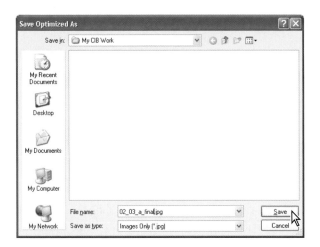

Note: If you do not see the My CIB Work folder, see "Saving a work file" on page 62.)

7 Repeat Steps 1-6 for the other two image files, saving them as **02_03_b final.jpg** and **02_03_c final.jpg**. You can then close your three original work files, saving them in Photoshop (PSD) format in the My CIB Work folder.

Converting the file to JPEG format flattens it so that the text effect and the original image are merged into one layer. By posting such an image on a Web site, you not only reduce the file size by using JPEG compression, you make the image viewable while protecting your rights to your image.

Congratulations, you've completed this project, so you can save and close any open files. In this project, you've created a new Photoshop (PSD) format document without an image and added text to that document. You've copied a layer from that document to other image files by dragging from the Layers palette to the image windows. You've used the Styles And Effects palette to apply an Effect to a text layer and experienced the difference that simplifying a text layer makes.

Project 4: Using Layer Styles and distortions

One of the key concepts introduced in Project 3 was simplifying a text layer—converting it to art so that you could apply artistic effects to the character shapes. After you simplified the text, you could no longer edit it with the Type tool.

That doesn't mean that you can't apply dramatic changes to text as text. You can. In this project, you'll create two versions of the finished image. In one, you'll simplify the text, but in the other, you'll get similar results without simplifying.

Your goal in this project is to create title text over an image, as if this were going to be used as a title page or cover for a calendar, magazine article, web page, or book.

Adding the subject text

Your first task is to find and open the image file for the project. Then, you'll add the text, which is probably a comfortable process for you from doing the previous three projects in this lesson.

1 Click Photo Browser (⌕) to switch to Organizer. If the Back To All Photos button appears above the thumbnails, select it now.

2 On the Tags tab, click the Find boxes for the Lesson 2 and Project 4 tags to find the image thumbnail for this project (a sports fisherman).

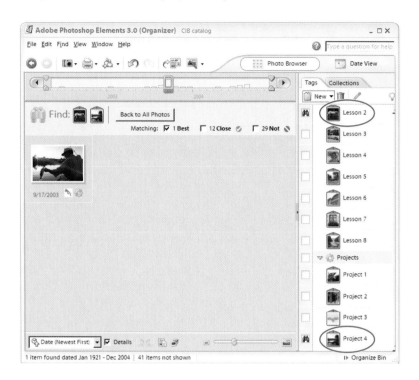

3 Select the thumbnail. Then click Edit (⬛) in the shortcuts bar, and choose Go To Standard Edit from the pop-up menu.

4 In the toolbox, select the Type tool (T) and make selections from the pop-up menus in the tool options bar to set the following attributes.

- For the font family, select any one of the heavier sans serif font families available on your computer, such as Arial Black.

- For the font style, select Bold, if it is available. Otherwise, leave the font style as is.

- For the font size, type **144 pt**.

- For text alignment, select Center text (≣).

- For leading (⫟), type **112 pt**.

5 Click the Type tool near the center of the image and type **FISHY**. Press Enter (on the main part of the keyboard, not in the numeric keypad) to create a line break, and type **TAILS**.

6 Click Commit (✔) in the tool options bar to accept the text.

7 If necessary, use the Move tool to drag the text into place.

Warping text

Stretching and skewing the text into unusual shapes is incredibly easy in Photoshop Elements 3.0. Make sure that the Type tool is selected before you begin.

1 In the Layers palette, select the FISHY TAILS text layer.

Note: It isn't necessary to highlight the text in the image window. You could do so, but it won't make a difference in this procedure because warping it applies to the entire layer.

2 On the tool options bar, click Warp Text (工), which opens the Warp Text dialog box.

3 In the Style pop-up menu, select Fish. (Avoid accidentally selecting Fisheye.) Then click OK to close the dialog box.

4 Click Commit (✔) in the tool options bar.

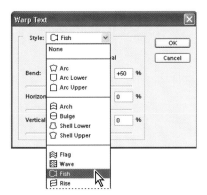

Stylizing and editing the text

In Project 3, you applied an Effect to text, which required you to simplify the text in the process. In this procedure, you'll use the Styles And Effects palette again, but this time you'll apply a Layer Style instead of an Effect. Layer Styles don't require simplified text.

1 In the Layers palette, make sure that the FISHY TAILS text layer is still selected, or select it now. If Commit (✔) still appears in the tool options bar, select it.

2 In the Styles And Effects palette, choose Layer Styles and Complex on the pop-up menus.

3 Scroll down the palette to the last thumbnail, Sunset Sky, and double-click it to apply the style to the selected layer, FISHY TAILS.

The Layer Style not only gives the text variegated color, but it adds a bevel and a drop shadow, giving it a raised, three-dimensional look.

4 Using the Type tool (T), click and drag to select the "IL" in the word *TAILS*.

Note: If you have trouble with this step, make sure that the Type tool is selected in the toolbox and the FISHY TAILS layer is selected in the Layers palette. Then try again.

5 Type to change the word *TAILS* to **TALES**. Then click Commit (✔) on the tool options bar.

Did you catch the significance of the last steps? In spite of the dramatic changes to the appearance of the text, you can still edit it as text. This affords you maximum flexibility to make editorial changes to your work file at a later date without having to redo the work.

Creating an unstylized copy of the text layer

The introduction to this project said that you would create two versions of the finished artwork. What it failed to mentioned is that you're going to create those versions on separate layers of the same work file instead of creating two work files.

1 In the Layers palette, select the text layer. Then click More to open the palette menu, and choose Duplicate Layer. Or, drag the text layer to the New Layer icon (⬛) in the Layers palette. (Accept the default layer name, FISHY TALES Copy.)

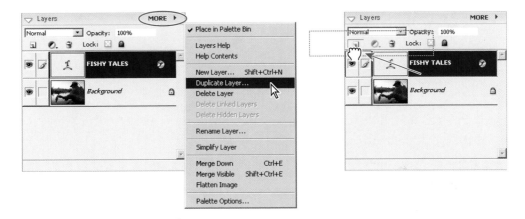

2 Click the eye icon (👁) beside the original FISHY TALES layer to make that layer invisible in the image window. (You won't see any difference in the image window because the two text layers are identical and perfectly aligned, one above the other.)

3 In the Layers palette, make sure the FISHY TALES Copy layer is selected and choose Layer > Layer Style > Clear Layer Style.

The warped text now appears in solid black, as it did before you applied the Layer Styles.

Simplifying and applying a pattern to text

You're now ready to add a different look to the copy of the text layer. Make sure that FISHY TALES Copy is selected in the Layers palette before you begin.

One of the interesting things you'll do in this procedure is to lock the transparent pixels on a text layer. This enables you to do all sorts of painting on the existing shapes in the layer without having to be careful to avoid the edges.

1 Using the Type tool, drag to select all the black FISHY TALES text (or, click the text once to place a cursor in it and then choose Select > All).

2 Click the arrow by Color in the tool options bar to open a Color Swatches palette, and select White as the text color. Click anywhere outside the palette to close it.

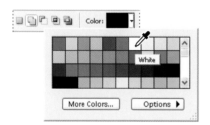

3 In the toolbox, hold down the mouse button on the Clone Stamp tool (⬛) until you can see the list of tools, and select the Pattern Stamp tool (⬛).

Or, you can select the Clone Stamp tool and then select the Pattern Stamp tool icon in the tool options bar.

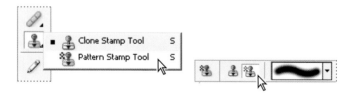

4 In the tool options bar, select the following:

• For Size, select **100 px** to set the diameter of the Pattern Stamp tool brush, either by typing or by clicking the arrow to open the slider and dragging to change the size.

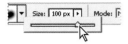

• For Mode, make sure that Normal is selected.

• For Opacity, make sure that 100% is selected.

• Make sure that the Bubbles pattern is selected. (Bubbles is the default pattern.)

Note: If you do not see the Bubbles thumbnail, click the arrow to open the Pattern Picker, choose either Default or Patterns in the pop-up menu, and then double-click the Bubbles thumbnail to select it and close the palette.

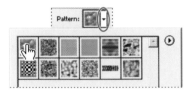

5 Try to drag the Pattern Stamp brush over the black FISHY TALES text. When a message appears, asking if you want to simplify the layer, click OK, but do not start dragging again yet.

6 In the Layers palette, select Lock Transparent Pixels (▨) to prevent changes to the transparent areas of the simplified FISHY TALES layer.

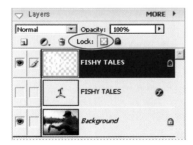

Notice that there is now a lock icon on the upper FISHY TALES layer, reminding you that you've applied a lock.

7 Paint with the Pattern Stamp tool, applying the pattern as solidly or unevenly as you like.

The pattern affects only the selected layer (the simplified text) and doesn't change any unselected layer (the underlying photograph). Also, because the transparent pixels on the FISHY TALES layer are locked, they also are protected, so only the simplified text shapes take on the pattern.

Simplifying the text layer, as you've done here, makes it impossible to edit it with the Type tool. However, you can add dimension to the patterned text by applying a Layer Style, such as a Bevel or Inner Glow, using the Styles And Effects palette.

Hiding and revealing layers to review the two versions

You'll use eye icons in the Layers palette to alternately show and hide the two layers with the FISHY TALES message.

1 In the Layers palette, make sure that the eye icons appear in the Layers palette for the Background layer and the upper FISHY TALES layer that you just painted with the Pattern Stamp tool.

2 Click the eye icon for the top layer, FISHY TALES, to remove that icon and hide the patterned text layer in the Layers palette.

3 Click the empty eye-icon box for the middle FISHY TALES layer, to place an eye icon and reveal the text layer with Sunset Sky as the Layer Style.

4 Change the visibility back and forth between the two layers until you decide which one you like better. Leave that layer showing and hide the other FISHY TALES layer.

5 Choose File > Save, and save the file as **02_04_Work.psd** in your My CIB Work folder you created earlier in this lesson. If Save In Version Set With Original is selected, be sure to deselect it before you click Save. Then close the file (choose File > Close).

You can add this project to your list of accomplishments for the day. In this section, you've applied a Layer Style to text that you warped, which leaves it fully editable but gives it some color and flair. You've learned how to create duplicate layers by either dragging or using a menu command and how to remove a Layer Style—something you can't do to an Effect in the same way. You've seen how locking transparent pixels on a layer helps you preserve the margins of the visible areas. Finally, you've kept two potential versions of the final art in one work file.

Project 5: Using Layer Styles and creating an animation

You don't need a video camera to create an animation. In this exercise, you're going to create a simple animation showing an entirely virtual neon sign flashing off and on in front of another image. As you'll discover, it's not that difficult to do.

You can create animations that have nothing to do with text. You can have animations that have more than two frames to make the changes more gradual. You can create an animation that plays only once or one that loops endlessly for as long as it is open. All that matters is how you prepare the layers and how you save the file.

Original

Animation frame 1

Animation frame 2

Setting up layers for the project

In the Layers palette, a lock icon always appears on the Background layer and the word *Background* is always shown in italics. That's because the Background layer is special and carries certain limitations on what you can do to it.

In this project, you'll want to make some changes that are not allowed on the Background layer. Consequently, you need to unlock that layer. You unlock an ordinary layer by selecting it and then selecting the lock icon at the top of the Layers palette. This won't work with the Background layer. Amazingly enough, you can unlock it simply by changing its name.

1 Using the techniques you've used in the four other projects in this chapter, switch to Organizer and use the Lesson 2 and Project 5 tags in Organizer to find, select, and open the 02_05.jpg file in Standard Edit.

2 Create a duplicate of the Background layer, using any one of the following three techniques:

• Choose Layer > Duplicate Layer, and click OK to accept the default layer name.

• In the Layers palette, drag the Background layer thumbnail to the New Layer icon.

• Click the More arrow in the Layers palette to open the palette menu, and choose Duplicate Layer. Accept the default name by clicking OK.

Two layers are stacked in the Layers palette: Background and Background Copy. Only the Background layer has the lock icon (🔒).

3 Double-click the Background layer to open the New Layer dialog box. Click OK to accept the default name, Layer 0.

The lock no longer appears on Layer 0 (the former Background layer).

You're going to need these two, editable copies of the original layer. They will serve as the basis for the two-frame animation.

Adding and arranging text layers

The process of adding and duplicating text layers is practically old hat to you at this stage of the lesson work. In this procedure, you'll do something new: Rearrange the stacking order of the layers.

1 In the Layers palette, select the Background Copy layer.

2 Select the Type tool (T), and use the tool options bar to select Arial Black (or another heavy, sans serif font family), Bold font style (if available), and **280 pt** for Size.

3 Click near the center of the image and type **EAT**. Click Commit (✓) on the tool options bar or press Enter on the numeric keypad to accept the typing.

4 Select the Move tool (✦✛) and drag the text as needed to center it in the image window.

5 In the Layers palette, drag the EAT text layer to the New Layer icon to create a copy of the text layer, EAT copy. Or, choose Layer > Duplicate Layer, and accept the default name.

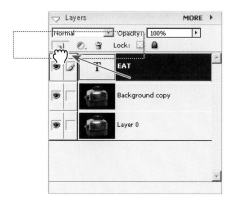

6 In the Layers palette, select the Background Copy layer and drag it upwards into position between the EAT and the EAT Copy layers.

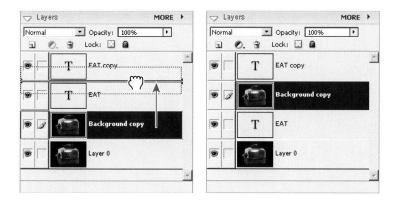

Adding neon effects to text

Your Layers palette is set up with alternating versions of the toaster image and the EAT text. So far, this doesn't seem too practical because all you can see are the upper text layer and Background Copy, which block your view of the lower text layer and Layer 0.

In this procedure, you'll apply Layer Styles that give the two text layers very different looks.

1 In the Layers palette, select the upper text layer, EAT Copy.

2 In the Styles And Effects palette, select Layer Styles and Wow Neon on the two pop-up menus.

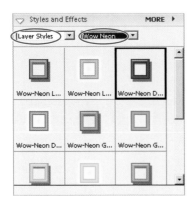

3 Scroll as needed to find Wow-Neon Dk Blue Off in the palette, and click that thumbnail once to apply it to the EAT copy layer.

Note: Be sure to select the Off *version of the Wow-Neon Dk Blue layer style. If you can't read the whole Layer Style name, let the pointer hover over a thumbnail until a tool tip appears identifying it. Or, click More at the top of the palette to open the palette menu, and select List View.*

4 In the Layers palette, click the eye icons (👁) for the EAT copy layer and the Background copy layer to hide them in the image window.

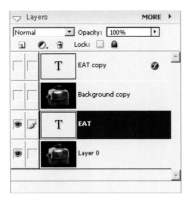

5 Select the EAT layer.

6 In the Styles And Effects palette, do both of the following:

• Click the Wow-Neon Red On thumbnail to apply it to the selected layer, EAT.

• Click the Wow-Neon Red Off thumbnail to apply it to the EAT Layer, too.

 Adding a second Layer Style does not replace the first one but enhances it in interesting ways.

Merging layers in preparation for animating

Although the text looks like art, it's not. It's still editable with the Type tool. For example, you could use the Type tool to change the word from EAT to ATE on the individual layers. But that flexibility will end abruptly during this procedure.

Because of this, it's a good idea to create a copy-—just in case you might need to change the file later and don't want to have to start again from the beginning.

1 Choose File > Save As, and use the Save As dialog box to name it **02_05_Work.psd.** Save it in the My CIB Work folder that you created earlier, with Photoshop (PSD) selected for Format. If Save In Version Set With Original is selected, be sure to deselect it before you click Save.

2 Choose File > Duplicate, and type **02_05_Merged** in the Duplicate Image dialog box, and click OK. Close the original work file, 02_05_Work.

3 In the Layers palette, click to set eye icons (☻) for the Eat Copy and Background Copy layers, making them visible again, and then select the EAT Copy layer.

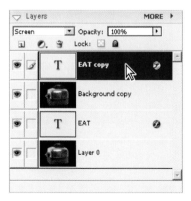

4 Choose Layer > Merge Down to flatten the EAT Copy and Background Copy layer.

Note: If the Merge Down command is unavailable (dimmed), make sure that you have the EAT Copy layer selected in the Layers palette and that both the EAT Copy and Background Copy layers have eye icons ( ) in the Layers palette. Then try again.

5 Select the EAT layer in the Layers palette, and again choose Layer > Merge Down to flatten the text layer with Layer 0.

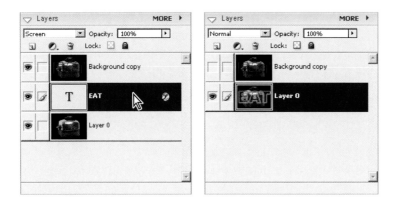

6 Choose File > Save. Then click Save in the Save As dialog box without making any further changes.

This process reduces the file to two layers, one with blue neon EAT text superimposed on the toaster image and one with glowing red neon EAT text on the same toaster image. You can see the two layers by clicking the eye icon for the upper layer off and on to show it or hide it, revealing the lower layer.

Animating the two layers

You've actually completed the most difficult phases of this project. Now here comes the fun part, creating the animation. It's shockingly simple, as you're about to discover.

1 With the 02_05_Merged file still active, make sure that both the Background Copy and Layer 0 layers are visible, or click to set eye icons ( ) for the layers.

2 Choose File > Save For Web.

3 In the Preset pop-up menu, choose GIF 128 No Dither. Then select Animate.

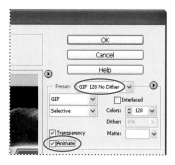

4 Under Animation, select Loop (if necessary), and select **1.0** seconds in the Frame Delay pop-up menu. (If the Animation options are not available, make sure that you selected Animate in the Preset area of the dialog box. See Step 3.)

5 Under New Size, do all of the following in this order:

• Select Constrain Proportions.

• In Width, type **320** pixels.

• Click Apply, and notice the reduced file size and download times listed under the optimized version of the image.

Note: After you click Apply, you can't undo this change. If you decide that the file size and quality are too low, click Cancel to close the Save For Web dialog box and start again.

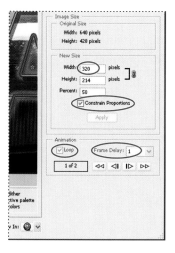

6 Review all settings, and click OK. In the Save Optimized As dialog box, type **EAT_anim.gif** as the file name, and click Save to save it in the My CIB Work folder.

7 Save and close the 02_05_Merged file. In Windows, click Start and choose Documents > EAT_anim.gif.

Or, locate the EAT_anim.gif file in Windows Explorer and double-click it.

The animation opens in your default application for viewing .gif files, such as Windows Image And Fax Viewer or your Web browser. When you finish enjoying your animation, close the viewer and return to Photoshop Elements.

Once again, congratulations. You've completed the final project in Lesson 2. In this one, you've dragged layers to change the stacking order in the Layers palette. You've unlocked the Background layer by changing its name. You've applied multiple Layer Styles to different layers, and you've merged two layers into one—twice! Finally, you've completed one of the possible uses of the Save For Web dialog box.

Organizing your finished project files

You've finished all the editing work for this lesson. Now, you'll do a simple follow-up task that will make it easy to find your work files again.

In every Save, Save As, and Save Optimized As dialog box, the Include In Organizer option is selected by default. That means that all your work files should be listed in your CIB Catalog for easy access and retrieval. If you do this now, before you work on other images, tagging the images is very simple indeed.

1 Click Photo Browser (⬚) on the Photoshop Elements shortcuts bar to switch to Organizer. If Back To All Photos appears above the thumbnails area, select it.

2 In the Tags palette, choose New > New Category on the pop-up menu.

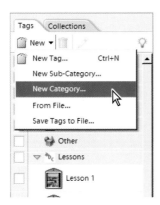

3 In the Create Category dialog box, type **Work Files** as the Category name, and select one of the Category icons (you can scroll to the right to see other icons). Click OK.

4 Choose Find > Untagged Items.

Since all the original images in the catalog are already tagged, only your own saved work files appear in the thumbnails now.

5 Choose Edit > Select All or press Ctrl + A to select all the thumbnails.

6 Drag the Work Files tag to the thumbnails to apply it. Leave all the thumbnails selected.

7 Expand the Lessons tag category, and drag the Lesson 2 tag to the thumbnails.

Whether or not you want to add the appropriate project number tags to the individual files is up to you. It's not necessary for later lessons in this book, but you certainly could do that if you want to. Or, you could create other tags and apply them.

You can now select Back To All Photos to see the entire catalog of thumbnails.

How to add missing work files to Organizer

If some of your work files weren't automatically added to Organizer when you saved them, you can add them to the CIB Catalog. You can use the following procedure or one of the other techniques you learned about in Lesson 1.

1. In Organizer, choose File > Get Photos > From Files And Folders.

2. In the dialog box that appears, locate and select the My CIB Work folder, and then do one of the following:

* *Click Get Photos to add everything in the folder to Organizer.*

* *Open the My CIB Work folder and select the file you want to add to the catalog. Or, Ctrl+click to select multiple files. Then click Get Photos.*

3. If messages appear saying that some of these files are already in the catalog, click OK.

4. Add the appropriate tags to the thumbnails, as needed.

5. Click Back To All Photos

If you get other error messages when you try to use files selected in organizer, see the Index for listings under "error messages."

Congratulations—you've finished this lesson on using text in Photoshop Elements.

You can review and test your mastery of the concepts and techniques presented here by working on the review questions on the next page.

Review questions

1 What is the advantage of having text on a separate layer?

2 Where is the tool options bar? How is it different from the toolbox?

3 What is a palette?

4 How do you hide a layer without removing it?

5 In the Layers palette, what do the lock icons do and how do they work?

Review answers

1 Because the text remains separate from the image, Photoshop Elements text layers can be edited in later work sessions, just like most other kinds of text documents.

2 The *toolbox* is the collection of tool icons. In the standard work area arrangement, it appears as a single column of icons along the left edge of the work area. The *tool options bar* appears across the top of the work area, just below the menus and shortcuts bar. The tool options bar shows the various settings you can select for the active tool. For example, when you select the Type tool, the tool options bar displays options for the fonts, text color, and so forth. When you select a different tool, the settings for that tool replace the text tool options in the tool options bar.

3 A palette is a floating window containing controls for functions that are not tied to a particular tool. For example, the Layers palette shows you the layer structure in the file and provides various options you can select to control how the layers work. The Navigator palette gives you easy access to alternate ways to zoom and scroll within an image. Neither of these functions is limited by which tool is currently active. You can open unseen palettes by selecting them on the Window menu. The Palette Bin provides handy access to your most frequently used palettes.

4 You can hide a layer by clicking the eye icon (👁) next to that layer on the Layers palette. To make the layer visible again, click the empty box where the eye icon should be to restore it.

5 Lock icons prevent changes to a layer. You can click Lock All (🔒) to lock all the pixels on the selected layer, or you can click Lock Transparent Pixels (▨) to protect only those areas. To remove a lock, select the locked layer and click the active lock icon to toggle it off. (This does not work for the Background layer, which can be unlocked only by renaming it to convert it into an ordinary layer.)

3 | Adjusting Color in Images

Photoshop Elements 3.0 equips you with many ways to shift colors around in your images. You'll find everything from automatic fixes that do an unbelievably good job on most photos to sophisticated hands-on tools that give you total control over what happens in your images.

In this lesson you can learn how to do the following:

- Auto-correct images from either Quick Fix or Standard Edit mode.

- Use individual auto options to improve images.

- Apply the Color Variations feature to shift color balance.

- Fix eyes that are discolored by a reflection of a camera flash.

- Replace the color of a pictured object with another color.

- Make and edit a selection area.

- Save a selection area for future use.

- Troubleshoot common problems in using Photoshop Elements 3.0.

This lesson shows you many different ways to change the color balance in your pictures, beginning with the seemingly magical, one-step correction features. From there, you'll go on to see for yourself that advanced features and adjustment techniques are not difficult to master, especially as you become more and more skilled in creating selections and using layers to accomplish your goals.

Most people need at least an hour and a half to complete the work in this lesson. The work involves four, independent projects, so you can do them all in one session or in several.

This lesson assumes that you are already familiar with the overall features of the Photoshop Elements 3.0 work area and recognize the two ways in which you can use Photoshop Elements: Editor and Organizer. This lesson focuses primarily on Editor. Lesson 3 also builds on the skills and concepts covered in Lessons 1 and 2. If you need to learn more about these items, see Photoshop Elements Help and the *Adobe Photoshop Elements 3.0 Getting Started Guide*.

If you haven't already copied the project files from the CD attached to the inside back cover of this book, do so now. See "Copying the Classroom in a Book files" on page 3.

Note: As you gather advanced skills in Photoshop Elements 3.0, you may sometimes experience more advanced difficulties. For help with common problems you might have when doing the projects in this book, see "Why won't Photoshop Elements do what I tell it to do?" on page 130.

Getting started

Before you start working on files, take a few moments to make sure that your work area and palettes are set up to match the illustrations shown for these projects.

1 Start Photoshop Elements in Standard Edit mode, either by selecting Edit And Enhance Photos in the Welcome screen as you start Photoshop Elements, or, if Organizer is already open, by clicking the Edit button ( ) and choosing Go To Standard Edit.

2 Use the Standard Edit ( ) and Quick Fix ( ) buttons to switch back and forth between these modes. Compare your Palette Bin arrangements to the illustrations below.

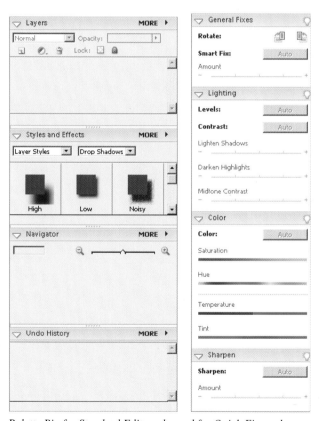

Palette Bin for Standard Edit mode, and for Quick Fix mode

In Standard Edit, you want only the Layers, Styles And Effects, Navigator, and Undo History palettes—the order is not important. In Quick Fix, expand any collapsed palettes by clicking the arrow beside the palette name on the palette title bar.

Note: For instructions on how to add or remove palettes from the Standard Edit Palette Bin, see "Using the Palette Bin" on page 59. (You can't add or remove palettes for Quick Fix mode.)

Now your Palette Bins are set up in both modes for the work you'll do in this lesson. In some procedures, you'll use Quick Fix mode and in others you'll use Standard Edit mode, so it's convenient to set them up ahead of time in the way you'll want them.

Fixing photographs automatically

You've probably noticed that not all the photographs used for the projects are of professional quality. But just because a snapshot isn't objectively great, that doesn't mean it's not valuable to you or doesn't deserve to be made as good as it can be. Many photographs selected for this book typify some of the challenges ordinary people with modest camera skills might face in attempting to make the most of pictures they want to keep.

Auto-fixing multiple files as a batch

Fixing files without even opening them? Yes, Photoshop Elements can do this. In this procedure, you'll apply automatic fixes to all the image files used in this lesson. You'll save those fixed files as copies of the originals so that you can compare the results at the end of each project.

1 Choose File > Process Multiple Files.

2 In the Process Multiple Files dialog box, set the source and destination folders as follows:

• For Process Files From, select Folder, if it is not already selected.

• Under Source, deselect Include All Subfolders. Then click Browse. Find and select the Lesson03 folder in the Lessons folder. Click OK to close the Browse For Folder dialog box.

• Under Destination, click Browse. Then find and select the My CIB Work folder that you created during Lesson 2 and placed in the Lessons folder. Click OK to close the Browse For Folder dialog box.

3 Select Rename Files. Type **Autofix_** in the first option, and select Document Name in the second option.

4 Under Quick Fix, on the right side of the dialog box, select all four options: Auto Levels, Auto Contrast, Auto Color, and Sharpen.

5 Review all selections in the dialog box, comparing them to the illustration below. Make sure that there are no check marks for the Resize Images or Convert Files To options.

Note: If an error message appears, saying that some files couldn't be processed, ignore it. This refers to a hidden file that is not an image, so it has no effect on the success of your project. If an error message appears saying that files are missing, that means that the Lessons folder has been moved or was not expanded correctly. See "Copying the Classroom in a Book files" on page 3 and redo that procedure, following the instructions exactly.

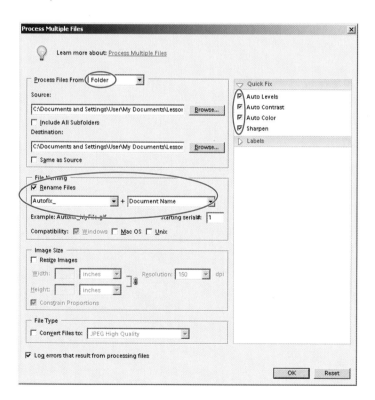

6 When you are sure that all selections are correct, click OK.

Photoshop Elements goes to work, automatically opening and closing image windows. All you need to do is sit back and wait for the process to finish.

Note: If you were expecting the files to be open at the end of the process, you just got a surprise, because they are not. You can see the auto-fixed images using Windows Explorer or in Photoshop Elements by choosing File > Browse Folders to open the File Browser. Then find and select the My CIB Work folder in the Folder palette so that the thumbnails for the auto-fixed files appear in the File Browser. For more information on the File Browser, see Photoshop Elements Help.

Adding the corrected files to Organizer

The Save, Save As, and Save Optimized As dialog boxes all have an Include In Organizer option that is selected by default. When you use the Process Multiple Files feature, this option isn't part of the process, so you must do that manually.

1 In Photoshop Elements, click Photo Browser (⟳) to open Organizer.

2 Choose File > Get Photos > From Files And Folders.

3 In the dialog box that appears, locate and open the My CIB Work folder.

4 Select the four Autofix_ files by holding down Shift or Ctrl as you click to select all four. Then select Get Photos.

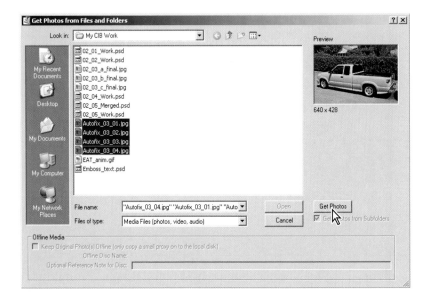

Organizer displays just the newly added image thumbnails. If a message appears reminding you that only the new photos will appear, click OK to close it.

5 Choose Edit > Select All, or press Ctrl + A.

6 Drag the Lesson 3 tag to add it to the thumbnails to apply it. Then drag the Work Files tag category to the thumbnails, too. (If you have not done Lesson 2, create the Work Files tag now. See "Organizing your finished project files" on page 96.)

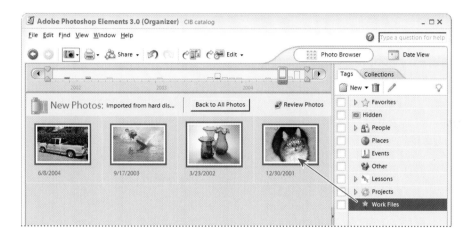

7 Select Back To All Photos.

Now your first set of results files are all set up, and you're ready to move on to other methods of correcting color.

Project 1: Applying individual auto adjustments

When you applied auto-fixes to the images using the Process Multiple Files dialog box, you never got to see any of the before, during, or after versions of the file. Although the automatic fixes give good results for many pictures, the process seems a bit mysterious.

In this project, you'll apply individual aspects of auto-fixing one at a time. This is useful because it shows you how the different phases affect the image and enables you to make individual adjustments to the correction process.

Opening image files for Quick Fix editing

You'll use the same technique you learned in Lesson 2 for using Organizer to find and open files for editing in Photoshop Elements.

The two images you'll work on are photographs of colored glass containers, one of which has an auburn color cast. You'll use the other for comparison, so that you can tell when your corrections do a good job of capturing the true colors of the glass objects.

1 If Organizer is no longer the active component, switch to it now.

2 On the Tags tab, click the Find box for the Lesson 3 tag in the Lessons category. Then click the Find box for the Project 1 tag in the Projects category.

3 Choose Edit > Select All.

4 Click Edit ( ) on the Organizer shortcuts bar, and choose Go To Quick Fix.

Unlike Standard Edit mode, the active image file always fills the entire work area.

5 In the View pop-up menu in the lower left area of the image window, choose Before And After (Portrait).

Note: You can change from Before And After (Portrait) to Before And After (Landscape) if that arrangement works better for you. The portrait view shows the before and after versions of the image side by side. The landscape view shows them one above the other.

Applying auto fixes one by one

You're about to see a step-by-step breakdown of the auto-fix process. Photoshop Elements should still be open in Quick Fix mode.

1 In the Photo Bin, select the 03_01.jpg thumbnail to make it the active file, if it is not already selected.

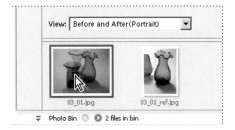

2 In the Palette Bin, under Lighting, select the Auto button for Levels. Notice the immediate effect on the image.

3 One at a time, select the Auto buttons for Contrast, Color, and Sharpen, noticing the difference in the image between each action.

4 Select Standard Edit (▨) on the shortcuts bar above the Palette Bin.

Note: If the active image takes up the entire work area, choose Window > Images > Maximize Mode to remove the check mark, which shifts the image display into Multi-window mode. Or, click the Multi-window mode button (⊡) on the far right of the Photoshop Elements menu bar.

5 Move the image windows so that you can see both the 03_01.jpg and the 03_01ref.jpg image, and compare the colors, using the 03_01ref.jpg image as a guide representing the true color of the purple vase.

6 Select the 03_01.jpg image that you corrected, and choose File > Save As.

7 In the Save As dialog box, locate and select the Lessons\My CIB Work folder, rename the file **03_01_Work**, and save it in JPEG format. If Save In Version Set With Original is selected, be sure to deselect it before you click Save. When the JPEG Options dialog box appears after you click Save, select High in the Quality pop-up menu, and click OK.

When you are ready to go on to the next project, close your files.

Project 2: Comparing methods of fixing color

The automatic correction features in Photoshop Elements 3.0 do an excellent job of bringing out the best in most photographs. But your photographs are unique, and so are the potential problems in the original photograph. Some photographs don't respond well to automatic fixes and require a more hands-on approach to color correction.

Photoshop Elements 3.0 offers many approaches to color correction. The more approaches you master, the more likely you'll be able meet the challenge of fixing a difficult photograph. In this project, you'll study three different procedures for correcting a color problem and compare the four results.

Creating extra working copies of an image

You're going to compare three approaches to color correction, so you'll need three copies of the same photograph.

By now, you're probably confident that you've mastered the procedure for using tags to locate the files you need in Photoshop Elements 3.0 Organizer. We agree. From now on, the instructions for opening files will be summarized rather than explained in detail.

1 Click Photo Browser ( ) on the shortcuts bar to switch to Organizer, and use the Lesson 3 and Project 2 tags to find the 03_02.jpg file, the photo of the waterskier.

2 Select the image thumbnail. Then click Edit ( ) and choose Go To Quick Fix.

3 In Quick Fix mode of Photoshop Elements Editor, choose File > Duplicate. When a message appears, click OK to accept the default name, 03_02 copy.jpg.

4 Repeat Step 3 to create another duplicate, 03_02 copy 2.jpg.

Leave all three copies of the image file open for the next topics. You can tell that all are open because the thumbnails appear in the Photo Bin.

Using only Color Auto fix

At the beginning of this lesson, you applied all four auto fixes to all the images for this lesson and saved the results in a separate location. Smart Fix is the equivalent of applying the same set of auto-fixes, but requires just one selection instead of four.

In this procedure, you'll apply just one type of auto-fix.

1 In the Photo Bin, select the 03_02.jpg thumbnail to make it the active file.

2 In the Color palette, click Auto to fix only the color.

3 Compare the Before and After views of the file.

4 Save the file (choose File > Save) in the Lessons\My CIB Work folder and in JPEG format, changing the name to **03_02_Work,** deselecting Save In Version Set With Original, and leaving all the other options in the Save and JPEG Options dialog box unchanged.

Adjusting the results of an auto-fix

In this procedure, you'll experiment with one of the sliders in the Quick Fix palettes.

1 In the Photo Bin, select the 03_02 copy thumbnail to make it the active file.

2 Click only the Auto button for Color. The results should be the same as you had in the previous procedure.

3 Drag the Temperature slider to the left a short distance.

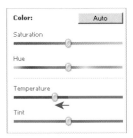

This cools down the image, enhancing the blue and green tones while reducing yellows, reds, and oranges.

4 Examine the results, paying particular attention to the skin tones and water colors.

5 As needed, readjust the Temperature slider until you are satisfied with the realistic balance between warm skin tones and cool water colors. Then click Commit (✔) on the Color-palette tab.

Note: If you aren't happy with the results and want to start over, click Cancel (⊘) on the Color palette tab. If you decide to undo the color fix after you click Commit, click the Reset button above the After view of the image. This restores the image to its original condition, so you can try fixing it again from the beginning.

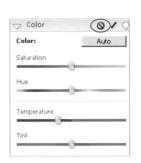

6 Save the file (choose File > Save) in the Lessons\My CIB Work folder and in JPEG format, changing the name to **03_02 copy_Work**. If Save In Version Set With Original is selected, be sure to deselect it before you click Save but leave the other options in the Save and JPEG Options dialog boxes unchanged.

Combining auto-fix and manual image corrections

The top four commands on the Enhance menu apply the same changes as the Auto buttons in Quick Fix. These commands are available in both Quick Fix and Standard Edit.

Both Quick Fix and Standard Edit offer other methods of enhancing color in images. These are found on submenus on the lower half of the Enhance menu. In this procedure, you'll use a manual option to tweak the results produced by an auto-fix button.

1 In the Photo Bin, select the 03_02 copy 2 thumbnail to make it the active file.

2 Again in the Color palette, click Auto to apply the automatic color correction.

3 Choose Enhance > Adjust Color > Color Variations.

4 In the lower left area of the dialog box, make sure that Midtones is selected and that the Amount slider is approximately centered. Then, do the following:

• Click the Increase Blue thumbnail once.

• Click the Decrease Red thumbnail once.

• Click OK.

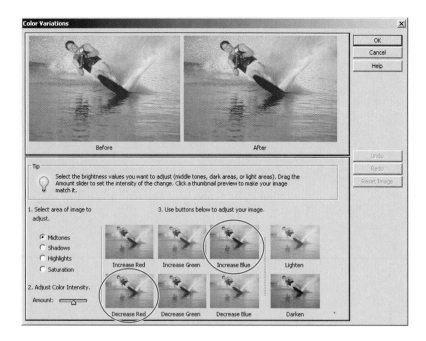

5 Choose File > Save As.

6 Save the file (choose File > Save) in the Lessons\My CIB Work folder and in JPEG format, changing the name to **03_02 copy 2_Work**. If Save In Version Set With Original is selected, be sure to deselect it before you click Save.

This combination of fixes gives the water a turquoise look and makes the swimming trunks electric green. To try a different combination, you can undo the changes and start again. (Choose Edit > Undo Color Variations, and then try again, starting with Step 4.)

Comparing results

At this point, all three copies of the image are open (as you can tell by looking at the Photo Bin). You'll compare them to the file you processed at the beginning of this lesson.

1 Choose File > Open. Locate and select the My CIB Work folder in the Lessons folder. Select the Autofix_03_02 file and click Open.

2 Select Standard Edit ( ) on the shortcuts bar to switch to that mode.

3 Choose Window > Images > Tile.

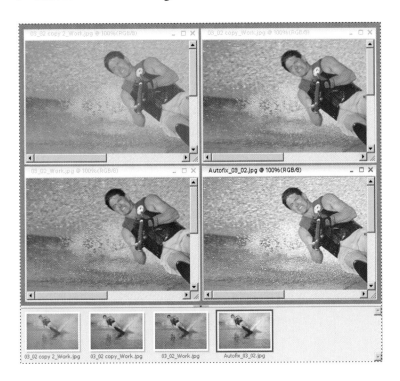

4 In the toolbox, select the Zoom tool ( ).

5 In the tool options bar, select Zoom Out (🔍), and then do one of the following:

• Click in the active image window until you can see the entire photo. Then choose Window > Images > Match Zoom.

• Select Zoom All Windows in the tool options bar, and then click in the active window.

💡 *Look for the highlighted thumbnail in the Photo Bin to see which file is active. Or, look at the title bars of the open image windows; the text is dimmed on inactive image windows but not dimmed on the active one.*

6 Examine the water, spray, skin tones, and clothing colors in the four versions. Decide which process you think did the best job. Then drag the corner edge of one of the image windows to resize it a little. (This turns off the automatic tiling for image windows.)

7 Choose File > Close All. When asked, do not save the changes.

There are even more ways to fix color that are well described in Help (choose Help > Photoshop Elements Help). Search Help for information about other commands on the Enhance > Adjust Color menu, such as Remove Color Cast and Hue/Saturation.

Project 3: Changing eye color in an image

Red eye occurs when a camera flash is reflected off the human retina so that the dark center of the eye looks bright red. The Red Eye tool (👁) is a simple, automatic, and highly convincing solution to this problem. The use of this tool is so easy and it is so well described in Help and in the How To palette, that there's little need to re-explain it here. If you have photographs that exhibit the red-eye phenomenon, you really owe it to yourself to check out the Red Eye tool on your own.

As smart as the Red Eye tool is, its use is limited to red eyes. You can't use it to make your brown eyes blue. It won't work for other colors of retinal reflections, such as the glowing eyes of an animal struck by a light beam or camera flash. Luckily for us, there's another tool that does the job almost as easily as the Red Eye tool.

Darkening reflective animal eyes

For this project, you'll use a flash photo of a cat. This picture is typical of the kind of retinal reflection that animal eyes produce in response to direct, strong light.

1 Using either Organizer or the File Browser, find the image file for this project (03_03.jpg) and open it in Standard Edit.

2 In the toolbox, do the following:

• Press D on your keyboard to set the colors to black and white. Or, click the Default Foreground And Background Colors icon, which is below the Foreground Color and Background Color swatches in the toolbox.

• Select the Color Replacement tool ( ) by holding down the mouse button over the Brush tool ( ) until the pop-up list appears, and selecting the Color Replacement tool.

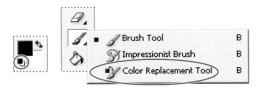

3 Use the pop-up menus, pop-up slider, or type to select the following items in the tool options bar: **13 px** as the Diameter (the default setting) in the Brush pop-up palette; Luminosity as the Mode; Once for Sampling; and 25% as the Tolerance.

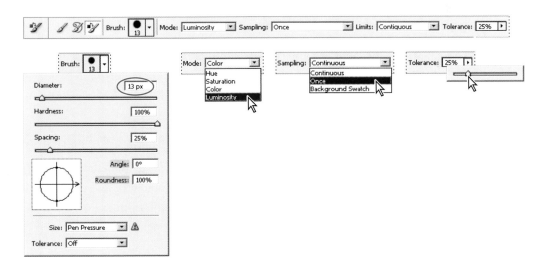

4 In the Navigator palette, drag the slider to the right to enlarge your view. Then drag the red frame to the cat's face in the thumbnail so that the cat's eyes are centered in the image and fill most of the image window.

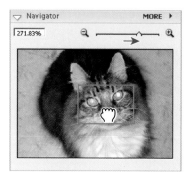

5 Center the Color Replacement tool over the upper part of the pupil on the left. Drag over that area of the eye without releasing the mouse button until black fills most of the pupil area (one small area should remain white, where there's a surface highlight).

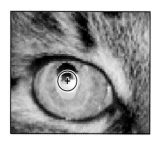

Note: Don't worry about keeping the brush within the shape of the pupil. If all the options described in Step 3 are in effect, the tool will replace only the brilliant yellow color reflected by the kitty's retina. If your results differ, review the tool options settings and try again.

6 Move the crosshairs over the right eye and drag over that pupil to make it solid black.

The Navigator palette is an easy way to zoom and scroll around in the image. The beauty of this feature is that you don't have to switch to the Zoom tool and then back to your editing tool. Dragging the red frame to the area you want to see is considerably quicker than doing vertical and horizontal scrolling. This method also helps you keep oriented about what part of the image you're seeing at very high zoom levels.

For some numerical options, you can change the value by scrubbing. *To scrub, move the pointer over the label (such as* Size *or* Tolerance *for the Color Replacement tool), so that the pointer changes shape ( ). Drag the pointer left or right across the label to make the number larger or smaller.*

What is a selection?

Project 3 in Lesson 3 introduces the process of creating selection areas. Ordinarily, the entire image area can be altered by the changes you apply to an image or image layer. That's because the whole image is active. A selection is a portion of the image area that you designate as the only active area of the image. When a selection is active, any changes you apply affect only the area within the selection; the rest of the image layer is protected, or masked.

Several tools can create selections, and you'll get experience with almost all of them in the course of doing the lessons in this book. Selections can be geometric in shape or free form, and they can have crisp or feathered edges.

Typically, a selection marquee—a border of dashed black and white lines that flashes—shows the boundaries of a selection. You can even save a selection to reuse at a later time. This can be a terrific time-saver when you need to use the selection several times.

For more information on selections, see Photoshop Elements Help.

Restoring the surface highlights

Unlike retinal reflections, reflections from the surface of the eye add realism and liveliness to a picture. The Color Replacement tool left the surface reflection in one of the cat's eyes. You'll take advantage of that by copying the reflection into the other eye.

1 In the toolbox, select the Elliptical Marquee tool ( ), which is grouped with the Rectangular Marquee tool ( ).

2 Drag a selection marquee around the small, white reflection in the eye on the left, including some of the black area.

3 Zoom in even more so that the eye is very large. Then select the Move tool (⯭).

4 Move the pointer inside the selection so that it appears as a black arrowhead (▶); then hold down Alt and drag a short distance to create and move a copy of the selected area. Release Alt and drag the copied selection into the cat's other eye.

Note: Be careful not to drag one of the corner handles because this will enlarge and distort the selection instead of copying and moving it. If that happens, click Cancel (⊘) in the tool options bar and try again.

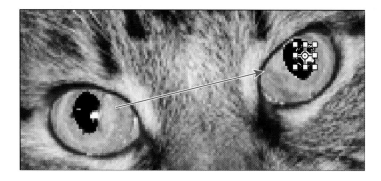

5 Deselect by choosing Select > Deselect or by pressing Ctrl + D.

6 Drag the slider in the Navigator palette to the left until you can see the entire image, and review the overall results.

7 Choose File > Save As. Save the file in the Lessons\My CIB Work folder and in JPEG format, changing the name to **03_03_Work**. (Keep Save In Version Set With Original deselected.) Choose File > Close, and then click OK in the JPEG Options dialog box.

Holding down the Alt key while you drag with the Move tool is a power-user technique. It's almost the same as copying and pasting except that copying and pasting places the copied area onto a separate layer. As you can see in the Layers palette, Alt-dragging left the copied pixels on the same layer as its source.

Congratulations, again. You've finished another project, which means there's only one more to go until you complete this lesson. In this project, you've learned how to use the Color Replacement tool for situations where the Red Eye tool can't produce the results you want. You've also learned a nifty shortcut for duplicating the image in a selected area by Alt-dragging with the Move tool.

About Sampling options for the Color Replacement tool

The Sampling option determines what colors will be changed by the Color Replacement tool. That color is determined by sampling the pixels that are directly under the crosshairs in the center of the brush shape. There are two types of sampling: Once and Continuous.

Once *Use this option to keep the sampling color the same throughout each stroke. For example, if the crosshairs are over a yellow area when you start to drag, then only yellow areas of the image will be changed as you continue the brush stroke across the image. If the crosshairs pass over a different color, the Color Replacement tool still changes only pixels matching the original yellow sample. This option is a good choice for changing small areas that don't have much variation in color, such as the cat's eyes.*

Continuous *Use this option to constantly resample as you move the Color Replacement tool. For example, if the position of the crosshairs is over a yellow area when you start to drag, and then the crosshairs pass over a red area, the Color Replacement tool will start out changing yellow pixels and then begin changing red pixels. The Continuous sampling option works better for large areas with shifts of color because you can release the mouse button from time to time. In this way, if you make a mistake and want to undo a step, you won't lose all your color replacement work, but just the most recent stroke.*

Project 4: Changing the color of a pictured object

Photoshop Elements offers two methods of swapping one color for another. The first is to use the Color Replacement tool, as you did in the previous project to replace yellow with black in the cat's eyes. You can use this technique to change any color to any other color—you're not limited to black—simply by changing the Foreground Color.

The second method is the one you'll use in this project. It's faster and more automatic than using the Color Replacement tool, but it doesn't work well for all types of images. This method is easiest when the color of the object you want to change is not found in other areas of the image. This color photograph of a bright yellow truck has very little yellow elsewhere in the image, making it a perfect opportunity for this approach.

Setting up layers and saving a selection

In this project, you'll change the color of the yellow truck. You'll do your work on a duplicate of the Background layer, which makes it easy to compare the finished project with the original picture.

In the previous project, you made your very first selection, which was of the highlight in the cat's eye. In this project, you're going to make a more difficult, free-form selection. As a safeguard, you're going to save the selection shape itself as a permanent part of the work file. Saving any complex selection is a good idea if there's any chance you may have to use it again, either to retrace your steps or to do something else with that selection.

1 Using the File Browser or Organizer, find the 03_04.jpg file, which is in the Lesson03 folder, and open it in Standard Edit mode.

2 Choose Layer > Duplicate Layer and accept the default name, or drag the Background layer to the New Layer icon in the Layers palette.

3 Select the Lasso tool (⌀) and drag it to draw a rough selection around the truck. It's OK if some of the road and background shrubbery are included in the selection.

Note: *The Lasso tool (⌀) is found in the toolbox with the Magnetic Lasso tool (⌀) and the Polygonal Lasso tool (⌀). You can quickly switch from one lasso tool to another by selecting it in the tool options bar instead of using the pop-up in the toolbox.*

4 In the tool options bar, select Subtract From Selection (⬚), and then drag a shape around some of the background greenery to remove it from the selection.

Note: It may be helpful to zoom in for this part of the process. Use the slider in the Navigator palette to zoom in so that you don't have to switch tools, or use the zoom-in keyboard shortcut, Ctrl + = (equal sign).

5 Continue to remove areas of greenery from the selection until the selection marquee fits reasonably well around the top of the truck—it doesn't need to be perfect, as long as all the truck is included.

6 Choose Select > Save Selection, and name the selection **Truck** before you click OK.

7 Press Ctrl + D to deselect, or choose Select > Deselect.

If you zoomed in for Step 4, you can zoom out now so that you can see the whole image.

Replacing a color throughout the image

A favorite thing about the Replace Color feature is that you don't have to be too careful when you apply it. In spite of that, you can produce spectacular results.

Fair warning: You're going to do this exercise twice. First you'll do it without loading the selection you saved. This will show you how much the color changes will affect the areas outside the truck, such as the landscaping.

1 In the Layers palette, select the Background Copy layer, if it is not already selected.

2 Choose Enhance > Adjust Color > Replace Color.

3 In the Replace Color dialog box, select Image so that you see the color thumbnail of the truck picture, and make sure that the Eyedropper tool (🖊) within the dialog box is selected. Then click a bright area of the yellow paint.

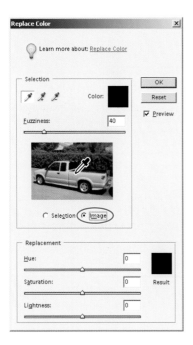

4 Click the Selection option under the thumbnail to see a black-and-white thumbnail, where white indicates the area that is selected.

5 Drag the Hue, Saturation, and Lightness sliders to change the color of the selected area. For example, try Hue = –60, Saturation = 8, and Lightness = –9 for a bright red.

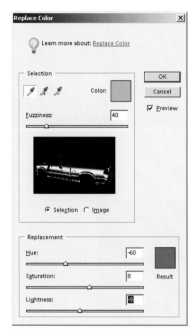

6 Adjust the color-application area by the following techniques:

• Select the Add To Sample () eyedropper, and click the thumbnail in an area corresponding to paint that still has a mustardy tinge to it.

• Drag the Fuzziness slider to the right until you reach an acceptable compromise between the color replacement on the truck and the effect the change has on the bushes in the background.

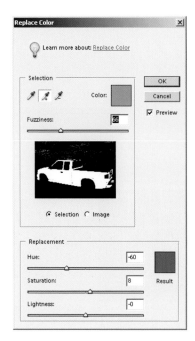

7 When you are satisfied with the results, click OK.

Depending on what color and color characteristics you used to replace the yellow, you probably can see a shift in the color of the shrubbery behind the truck. If this is a compromise you can live with, that's great. If not, you may need to try another technique, which is what you'll do in the next procedure.

Replacing a color in a limited area the image

You're going to try the previous procedure again, but this time you'll limit the affected area by loading a selection.

1 Choose Edit > Undo Replace Color, or select the step before Replace Color on the Undo History palette.

Note: If you can't stand the idea of permanently undoing your work, you can save a copy of the file, using the File > Duplicate command and saving the duplicate as another name. Or, using the original work file, you could create a new copy of the Background layer (Layer > Duplicate Layer), and then drag it to the top of the stack in the Layers palette so that you can see and work on just the new layer.

2 Choose Select > Load Selection. Make sure that Truck is displayed as the selection, and click OK.

3 Choose Enhance > Adjust Color > Replace Color.

4 Using the same techniques and settings you used in the previous procedure, make adjustments in the Replace Color dialog box to change the color of the truck. (See "Replacing a color throughout the image" on page 124, steps 3-6.)

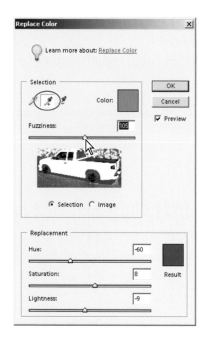

5 When you are satisfied with the results, click OK to close the dialog box.

6 Choose Select > Deselect, or press Ctrl + D.

7 Choose File > Save As, and save the file in the Lessons\My CIB Work folder. For File Name, type **03_04_Work**. Make sure that the Format option is Photoshop (PSD), or select that now. If Save In Version Set With Original is selected, be sure to deselect it before you click Save. After you've saved it, close the file.

Take a bow—you've finished the four projects in this lesson. In Project 4, you've learned how to make a selection with the Lasso tool. You've edited that selection to make it fit more closely, and you've saved it so that you can reload it on the image later or in future work sessions. You've then replaced one color with another using the Replace Color dialog box rather than the Color Replacement brush. In the process, you've also used the Undo History palette to step backwards to a specific point in your work.

Saving and organizing finished files

You'll use the tags you created in Lesson 2 to organize the new work files. These lesson files are a good opportunity to use the Stacking feature in Organizer, which makes reviewing and finding image files even easier.

1 If necessary, click Photo Browser (⊘▦) on the shortcuts bar to switch to Organizer. If the Back To All Photos button appears on the Organizer shortcuts bar, select it.

2 Choose Find > Untagged Items.

Thumbnails for the work files you created in this lesson are now the only ones you see.

3 Choose Edit > Select All or press Ctrl + A.

4 Drag the Work Files tag to the thumbnails to apply it. Repeat this step to add the Lesson 3 tag to the thumbnails.

5 Select the first waterskier thumbnail and then Shift-click the last waterskier thumbnail to select all four versions of this image. Or, if the waterskier images are not next to each other, hold down Ctrl and click each of the waterskier thumbnails. (All four will be highlighted by a blue outline.)

6 Choose Edit > Stack > Stack Selected Photos.

Now only one waterskier image appears, but it has a Stack icon (▤) in the upper right corner, indicating that other versions of this image are stacked with it.

7 Repeat Steps 4 and 5 for the two copies (work files and autofix files) of each of the other three projects: the cat, the vases, and the truck.

Why won't Photoshop Elements do what I tell it to do?

In some situations, the changes you try to apply to an image may not seem to work. Or, you may hear a beep sound, indicating that you're trying to do something that's not allowed.

The following list offers common explanations and solutions for what might be blocking your progress.

Commit is required *Several tools, including the Type tool (* T *) require you to click Commit (* ✔ *) in the tool options bar before you can move on to another task. The same is true when you crop with the Crop tool or resize a layer or selection with the Move tool.*

Cancel is required *The Undo command isn't available while you have uncommitted changes made with the Type tool, Move tool, or Crop tool, for example. If you want to undo those changes, click Cancel (* ⊘ *) in the tool options bar instead of using the Undo command or shortcut.*

Edits are restricted by an active selection *When you create a selection (using a marquee tool, the Magic Wand tool, or the Selection Brush tool, for example), you limit the active area of the image. Any edits you make will apply only within the selected area. If you try to make changes to an area outside the selection, nothing happens. If you want to deactivate a selection, choose Select > Deselect, and then you can work on any area of the image.*

Selection marquee around active area, erasure stroke

Move tool is required *If you drag a selection, the selection marquee moves, not the image within the selection marquee. If you want to move a selected part of the image or an entire layer, use the Move tool (* ▶⊕ *).*

Background layer is selected *Many changes cannot be applied to the Background layer. For example, you can't erase, delete, change the opacity, or drag the Background layer to a higher level in the layer stack. If you need to apply changes to the Background layer, double-click it and rename it (or accept the default name, Layer 0).*

Active layer is hidden *In most cases, the edits you make apply to only the currently selected layer—the one highlighted in the Layers palette. If an eye icon (👁) does not appear by that layer in the Layers palette, then the layer is hidden and you cannot edit it. Or, if the image on the selected layer is not visible because it is blocked by an opaque upper layer, you actually will be changing that layer but you won't see the changes in the image window.*

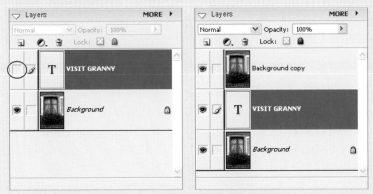

Hidden layer active, and layer view blocked by opaque upper layer

Active layer is locked *If you lock a layer by selecting the layer and then selecting the Lock (🔒) in the Layers palette, the lock prevents the layer from changing. To unlock a layer, select the layer and then select the Lock at the top of the Layers palette to remove the lock.*

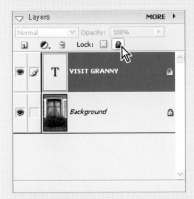

Locking or unlocking a layer

Wrong layer is selected (for editing text) *If you want to make changes to a text layer, be sure that layer is selected in the Layers palette before you start. If a nontext layer is selected when you click the Type tool in the image window, Photoshop Elements may create a new text layer instead of placing the cursor in the existing text layer.*

💡 *You can change which image appears at the top of a stack by selecting the stack thumbnail and choosing Edit > Stack > Reveal Photos In Stack. This limits the Organizer thumbnail display to just the images in that stack. Select the thumbnail you want to use, and choose Edit > Stack > Set As Top Photo. When you click Back To All Photos above the thumbnail area, the thumbnail you selected appears, representing the entire stack.*

About printing color pictures

Sometimes, pictures that look great on your computer don't turn out so well when you print them. How can you make them look as good in print as they do on screen?

Color problems in images can arise from a variety of sources. One may be the camera or the conditions under which the photograph was taken. If the photograph is flawed, then you can usually make it better by editing it with Photoshop Elements, as you did with the projects for this lesson.

There are other possible contributors to color problems. One may be your monitor, which may shift colors in ways that you are so used to that you don't notice. You can correct that by calibrating your monitor.

Another possibility is that your color printer interprets color information differently than your computer. You can correct that by activating the appropriate type of *color management* (choose Edit > Color Settings, and select the appropriate option in the dialog box if you know which one is appropriate for your needs).

Monitor calibration, color management, and the choices involved in these are discussed in a series of topics in Help. For more information, choose Help > Photoshop Elements Help and search for topics on these subjects.

Review questions

1 How do you go back and forth from Standard Edit mode to Quick Fix mode?

2 Can you apply automatic fixes when you are in Standard Edit mode?

3 What tool do you use to fix the red-eye phenomenon created by some flash cameras? Can you use the same tool to fix glowing animal eyes?

4 What is a selection?

5 Name two selection tools and describe how they work.

Review answers

1 When you work in Photoshop Elements 3.0 Editor, you can click Standard Edit ( ) and Quick Fix ( ) on the shortcuts bar to switch back and forth between the two editing modes.

2 Yes. The Enhance menu contains commands that are equivalent to the buttons in the Quick Fix palettes: Auto Smart Fix, Auto Levels, Auto Contrast, and Auto Color Correction. The Enhance menu also provides an Adjust Smart Fix command, which opens a dialog box in which you can change the amount of automatic fixing.

3 The Red Eye tool ( ) does an extraordinarily good job of automatically fixing red eye. However, it works only with red, not with the glowing yellow or green eyes that a camera flash or other strong light will create in an animal's eyes. To change animal eyes, you need to use other techniques, such as using the Color Replacement tool ( ), as described in Project 3 in this lesson.

4 A selection is an area you define as the only part of a layer that can be altered. The areas outside the selection are protected from change for as long as the selection is active.

5 The Elliptical Marquee tool ( ) and its close cousin, the Rectangular Marquee tool ( ) make selections in fixed geometric shapes when you drag them across the image. The Lasso tool can create free-form selections; you drag the Lasso tool around the area that you want to select. In later lessons in this book, you'll use the Magic Wand tool, which selects all the areas with the same color as the place where you click it. Another tool that you'll use in later lessons is the Selection Brush tool, which works like a paint-brush that you drag over the image to select areas.

4 | Fixing Exposure Problems

Did the flash fail to go off? You can fix that. Did bright reflections throw off the colors? Is the heirloom print almost faded beyond recognition? No problem. You can fix any of these—you and Photoshop Elements 3.0.

In this lesson you will learn how to do the following:

• Brighten underexposed photographs.

• Bring out details and colors in overexposed and faded photographs.

• Correct different areas of an image individually.

• Save selection shapes to reuse in later sessions.

• Create and apply adjustment layers.

Lesson 4 leads you through several approaches to correcting exposure problems in photographs. This aspect of color correction is often easier to fix than you might imagine.

Most users can complete this lesson a little over an hour.

This lesson assumes that you are already familiar with the overall features of the Photoshop Elements 3.0 work area and recognize the two ways in which you can use Photoshop Elements: Editor and Organizer. If you need to learn more about these items, see Photoshop Elements Help and the *Adobe Photoshop Elements 3.0 Getting Started Guide*. This lesson also builds on the skills and concepts covered in the earlier lessons.

If you are starting your work in this book at Lesson 4, make sure that you have already copied the project files from the CD attached to the inside back cover of this book. See "Copying the Classroom in a Book files" on page 3.

Also, see "Getting started" on page 105 of Lesson 3 for instructions on the work area arrangement on which the procedures are based.

Getting started

You'll start this lesson in the same way as you started your work in Lesson 3: by processing all the image files for this lesson at once to apply the automatic fixes available in Photoshop Elements 3.0. You'll save these files so that you can compare them to the files that you fix by setting options and other manual techniques.

1 Start Photoshop Elements in Standard Edit by selecting Edit And Enhance Photos on the Welcome screen. Or, if Organizer is open, click Edit (⬛) and choose Go To Standard Edit.

2 Choose File > Process Multiple Files.

3 In the Process Multiple Files dialog box, do the following:

• Choose Folder on the Process Files From pop-up menu.

• Under Source, select the Browse button, and then locate and select the Lessons\Lesson04 folder, and click OK.

• Under Destination, click Browse, and then locate and select the Lessons\My CIB Work folder.

• Select Rename Files. Type **Autofix_** in the first option, and select Document Name in the second option.

4 On the right side of the dialog box, select all four Quick Fix options: Auto Levels, Auto Contrast, Auto Color, and Sharpen. Review your settings, and then click OK.

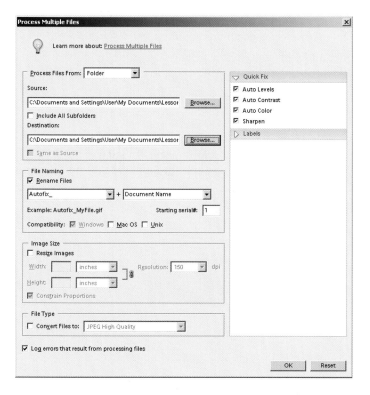

It takes a few seconds for Photoshop Elements to process the files. Image windows will open and close automatically as the changes are applied. There's nothing else you need to do. If an error message appears, click OK.

At the end of this lesson, you'll compare the results of this simple, automatic fixing of the images with the manual techniques. In many cases, this automatic type of fix is all you need to get the quality that you want.

Project 1: Brightening an underexposed image

A slightly underexposed photograph looks a little dingy and dull. For many such photos, the auto-fix lighting feature does a terrific job of brightening these up. Another method that's almost as easy as an auto-fix is the simple technique you'll use in this project.

In this lesson, the instructions tell you to use the File Browser to find and open files. You could use the Lesson and Project tags in Organizer instead to find the files, as you've done in Lessons 2 and 3. However, it's good to get some practice with alternate methods of locating files. The File Browser has its own menu bar and a set of palettes that you can expand, collapse, group, and rearrange by clicking or dragging the tab. File Browser palettes cannot float or be removed from the File Browser. See Photoshop Elements Help for more information.

1 Choose File > Browse Folders to open the File Browser.

2 In the Folders palette, find and select the Lesson 4 folder in the Lessons folder on your hard disk. Then select the 04_01.jpg thumbnail on the right side of the File Browser.

3 Open the file by doing one of the following inside the File Browser:

• Choose File > Open on the File Browser menu bar.

• Double-click the 04_01.jpg thumbnail.

• Double-click the image in the Preview palette in the File Browser.

4 Close or minimize the File Browser. Then do one of the following to duplicate the Background layer of the image:

• Choose Layer > Duplicate Layer, and click OK to accept the default name.

• Right-click Background in the Layers palette, and choose Duplicate Layer. Click OK.

• Drag the Background to the New Layer (⧉) shortcut at the top of the Layers palette.

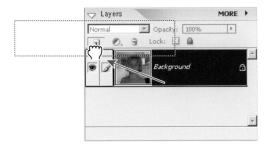

The new layer, Background Copy, is highlighted in the Layers palette because it is the selected (active) layer.

5 In the Layers palette, choose Screen as the blending mode, to replace Normal.

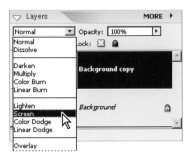

Note: If the pop-up menu shown above is not available, make sure that the Background Copy layer is selected in the Layers palette, not the original Background layer. You can't apply a blending mode to the Background.

6 Choose File > Save, and save the file as **04_01_Work.psd** in the Lessons\My CIB Work folder that you created in Lesson 2. Make sure that Save In Organizer is selected, and that you've deselected Save In Version Set With The Original.

If a message appears about maximizing compatibility, click OK to close it. Or, follow the instructions in the message to prevent it from appearing again.

7 When you finish viewing the results, close the file.

In this first project, you've seen how simple it is to use blending modes to brighten a dull image. You'll use other blending modes in other projects to correct different kinds of image problems. For more information about blending modes, see Photoshop Elements Help.

Project 2: Improving faded or overexposed images

In this project, you'll work with the scan of an old photograph (circa 1920s) that has faded badly and is in danger of being lost forever. Although it's not necessarily an award-winning shot, it could represent an era of personal history that you might want to preserve for future generations.

The automatic fixes you applied earlier in this lesson to a copy of this image improve the photograph quite a bit. In this project, you'll try to do even better using other techniques.

Creating a set of duplicate files

You're going to compare a variety of techniques during the course of this project. You'll start by creating individual files for each technique and giving them unique names. These names will help you identify the technique used to adjust each file.

1 Choose File > Browse Folders to reopen the File Browser. Using the same process that you used in the previous project, find, select, and open the 04_02.jpg file, which is in the Lesson04 folder. Then minimize or close the File Browser.

2 Choose File > Duplicate, and type **Shad_High** in the dialog box that appears to name the file, and click OK.

3 Repeat Step 2 two more times, naming one of the duplicate files **Bright_Con** and the other one **Levels**.

4 In the Photo Bin, select the 04_02.jpg thumbnail to make that image active.

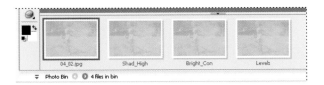

5 Choose File > Save As. When a dialog box appears, type **Blend_Mode** as the new file name and select Photoshop (PSD) in the Format pop-up menu. Select the Lessons\My CIB Work folder as the Save In location. If Save In Version Set With Original is selected, be sure to deselect it before you click Save. Click OK in any dialog boxes or messages that appear to accept the defaults.

6 Leave all four images open for the rest of the project.

Using blending modes to fix a faded image

This technique is similar to the one you used earlier to correct an underexposed image. In this case, you'll use other blending modes to fix this exposure problem.

1 In the Photo Bin, make sure that Blend_Mode.jpg is highlighted, or click that thumbnail to make it active.

2 Duplicate the Background layer (choose Layer > Duplicate Layer, or use one of the other techniques described in the previous project). Click OK in the dialog box that appears, to accept the default name, Background Copy.

Leave the Background Copy layer selected for the next step.

3 In the Layers palette, do both of the following:

• Choose Multiply on the blending modes pop-up menu.

• Drag the Background Copy layer to the New Layer icon (⬑) to create another duplicate, Background Copy 2.

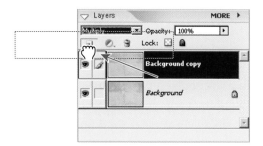

4 In the Layers palette, select the following options for the Background Copy 2 layer:

• Change the blending mode from Multiply to Overlay.

• Set the Opacity at about **50%**, either by typing or by dragging the Opacity slider.

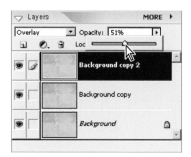

The Overlay blending mode cheers up the image considerably, but the image contrast is still unimpressive.

5 Select the Background Copy layer (not Background Copy 2), and choose Layer > Duplicate Layer. Click OK in the dialog box to accept the default name, Background Copy 3.

The new duplicate layer also has Multiply blending mode, which adds the extra bit of muscle this picture needs.

6 (Optional) Fine-tune the results by adjusting the Opacity settings for the individual layers until the image achieves a balance. (This is a judgment call, so you'll have to decide on your own what settings produce the best results.)

Note: You cannot change the Opacity of the locked Background layer.

7 Choose File > Save As, and save the file in the Lessons\My CIB Work folder. If Save In Version Set With Original is selected, be sure to deselect it before you click Save. Leave the file open.

Blending modes make layers interact with the layers under them in various ways. Multiply intensifies the dark pixels in an image. Overlay tends to brighten an image. For this project, using Overlay adds clarity and brilliance without cancelling out the effect of the Multiply blending mode on the underlying layers.

The stacking order of the layers makes a difference, so if you dragged one of the Multiply blending-mode layers to the top of the layer stack, you'd see slightly different results.

Adjusting shadows and highlights manually

Although both auto-fixing and blending modes do pretty good jobs of correcting the fading in this image, some of your own photos may be more challenging. You'll try three new techniques in the next three procedures.

The first technique involves using sliders for Shadows, Highlights, and Midtone Contrast.

1 In the Photo Bin, select the Shad_High thumbnail.

2 Choose Enhance > Adjust Lighting > Shadows/Highlights.

3 Select the Preview option in the Shadows/Highlights dialog box, if it is not already selected. If necessary, drag the dialog box aside so that you can also see most of the Shad_High image window.

By default, the Lighten Shadows setting is 50%, so you'll see a difference in the image already.

4 In the Shadows/Highlights dialog box, do all of the following:

- Drag the Lighten Shadows slider to the left to 30%, or type **30%**.

- Drag the slider or type to set Darken Highlights at **15%**.

- Drag the slider or type to set the Midtone Contrast at about **+30%**.

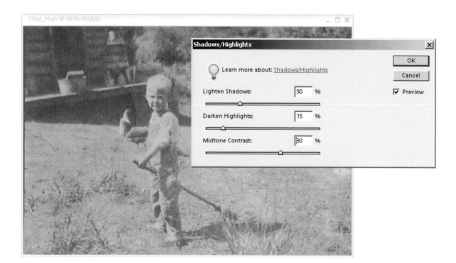

5 Readjust the three settings as needed until you think the image is as good as it can be. Then click OK to close the dialog box.

6 Choose File > Save As, and save the file in the Lessons\My CIB Work folder. If Save In Version Set With Original is selected, be sure to deselect it before you click Save. Then leave the file open.

The sliders you used in this technique are also available in the Lighting palette in Quick Fix mode. One of the differences between the two sets of sliders is that the dialog box version also displays numbers for the slider settings.

Adjusting brightness and contrast manually

The next approach for exposure problems uses another dialog box that you open from the Enhance > Adjust Lighting menu.

1 In the Photo Bin, select the Bright_Con thumbnail.

2 Choose Enhance > Adjust Lighting > Brightness/Contrast.

If necessary, drag the dialog box aside so that you can also see most of the Bright_Con image window.

3 In the Brightness/Contrast dialog box, do all of the following:

• Select Preview, if it is not already selected.

• Drag the Brightness slider to -30, or type **-30** in the box, being careful to include the minus sign when you type.

• Drag or type to set the Contrast at **+55**.

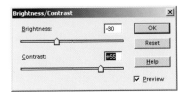

4 Adjust the Brightness and Contrast settings as needed until you think the image is as good as it can be. Then click OK to close the dialog box.

5 Choose File > Save As, and select the Lessons\My CIB Work folder as the location. If Save In Version Set With Original is selected, be sure to deselect it before you click Save. Click OK when the JPEG Options dialog box appears. Leave the file open.

Adjusting levels manually

Levels are the range of *color values*—the degree of darkness or lightness, regardless of whether the color in question is red, yellow, purple, or another color. In this procedure, you'll try to enhance the photograph by shifting the reference points for levels.

1 In the Photo Bin, select the Levels thumbnail.

2 Choose Enhance > Adjust Lighting > Levels.

3 Select the Preview option in the Levels dialog box, if it is not already selected.

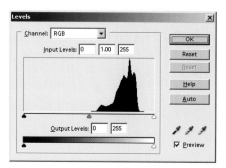

If necessary, drag the dialog box aside so that you can also see most of the image window for this file.

4 In the Levels dialog box, do all of the following:

• Drag the black arrow that is beneath the left side of the graph to the right and position it under the first steep spike in the graph shape. At that position, the value in the first Input Levels box is approximately 143.

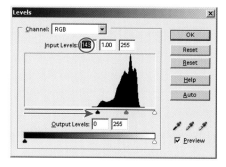

• Drag the white arrow on the right side of the graph until it reaches the edge of the final spike in the graph shape. The value of the third Input Levels box changes to approximately 225.

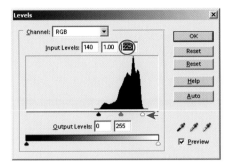

• Drag the gray center arrow under the graph towards the right until the middle Input Level value is approximately 0.90.

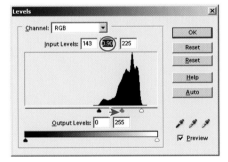

5 Adjust the arrow controls for the Levels graph as needed until you think the image is as good as it can be. Then click OK to close the dialog box.

6 Choose File > Save As, and save it with the others in the Lessons\My CIB Work folder. (If Save In Version Set With Original is selected, be sure to deselect it before you click Save.) Leave the file open after you click OK in the JPEG Options dialog box.

The graph represents the distribution of pixel values in the image. There are no truly white pixels or truly black ones. By dragging the sliders inward to where the pixels start to appear in the graph, you redefine what levels are calculated as dark and light. This enhances the contrast between the lightest pixels in the image and the darkest ones.

Comparing results for the various techniques

You can now compare the five versions of the image: these four and the one that you auto-fixed with the other project files at the beginning of this lesson. (If you have not already done that procedure, see "Getting started" on page 138.)

1 Using the File Browser, find and open the Autofix_04_02.jpg file in the Lessons\My CIB Work folder. Then close the File Browser.

2 In the Photo Bin, make sure that only the five files for this project are open: Autofix_04_02, Blend_Mode, Shad_High, Bright_Con, and Levels. Close any other open files.

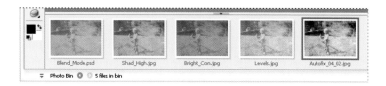

3 Click Automatically Tile Windows (▦) on the right side of the menu bar. Or, choose Window > Images > Tile.

Note: If you do not see the icon for tiling windows, make sure that you are in Standard Edit mode, not Quick Fix.

4 Do one of the following to reduce the zoom level for all active windows:

• Use the Navigator palette slider, Zoom tool, or View menu commands to change the zoom of the active image window. Leave the same image window active, and choose Window > Match Zoom and Window > Match Location to change all open images to the same zoom percentage and area of the image.

• Select the Zoom tool (🔍). In the tool options bar, select Zoom Out (🔍)and Zoom All Windows. Then click in the image window.

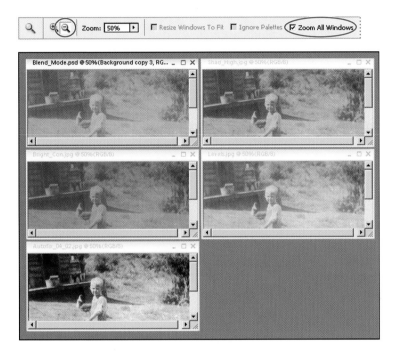

5 Compare the files, and decide which technique did the best job for you.

6 Click Automatically Tile Windows (⊞) again to deselect it. (You won't see any difference in the arrangement of image windows, but it will stop the automatic rearrangement when you open or close other images.)

7 Choose File > Close All.

Because your judgment and preferences are unique, your favorite of the five techniques you've tried in the project are bound to be unique, too. At a certain point, what creates the best-looking image is not just a question of skill, but also involves personal taste and your goals for using the image.

Congratulations—you've successfully completed another project. In doing so, you've used various automatic and manual approaches to correct overexposed photographs and scans of faded prints. You've tried auto fixes, blending modes, and the three dialog boxes that are available on the Enhance > Adjust Lighting submenu. You know that you can apply these different adjustments either separately or in combinations.

Project 3: Using adjustment layers to edit images

If you reopened one of the files from the previous project that used the Adjust Lighting submenu, you'd see that the values you entered in those dialog boxes no longer appeared. Instead, the starting point of the options would have shifted, so you could only guess at how to undo those and get back to your original starting point. This change took place as soon as you clicked OK in those dialog boxes, before you closed the file.

Sometimes that won't do. Sometimes, you need to go back and tweak your settings after the first adjustment, or even during a much later work session. Adjustment layers are a way of applying changes to layers that you can edit in a later work session.

Creating adjustment layers for lighting

In this project, you'll use a badly underexposed photograph of some flowering plants. It's hard to imagine that this picture could ever be useful, but Photoshop Elements can rescue many an otherwise hopelessly bad picture.

Before you begin, make sure that Photoshop Elements is open in Standard Edit mode and that the Layers palette is available in the Palette Bin.

1 Using the File Browser (File > Browse Folders), find and open the 04_03.jpg file. Or, switch to Organizer, find the only file with both the Lesson 4 and Project 3 tags; then click Edit (![icon]) on the shortcuts bar and choose Go To Standard Edit.

2 Choose Layer > New Adjustment Layer > Brightness/Contrast, or click Create Adjustment Layer (![icon]) on the Layers palette and choose Brightness/Contrast on the pop-up menu.

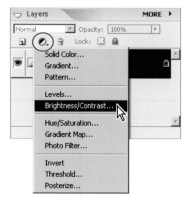

If a New Layer dialog box appears, click OK to accept the default name, Brightness/Contrast 1.

3 In the Brightness/Contrast dialog box, drag the sliders so that Brightness is 60 and Contrast is 30, and then click OK.

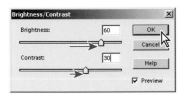

4 Repeat Step 2, but this time choose Levels (instead of Brightness/Contrast), so that the new layer will automatically be named Levels 1.

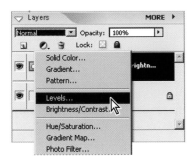

5 In the Levels dialog box, drag the black, white, and gray arrows that are under the graph to the left or right until the balance of dark and light areas looks right to you. (Our example uses values of 30, 1.2, and 155.)

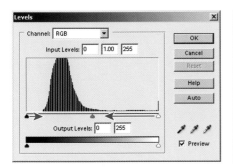
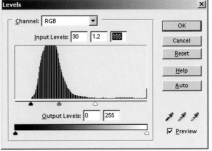

6 Click OK to close the Levels dialog box.

The beauty of adjustment layers is that you can revert to earlier settings, even in later work sessions, as long as you save the file in Photoshop (PSD) format (the default). For example, if you double-click the Layer thumbnail for the Brightness/Contrast 1 layer, your original settings (+60 and +30) still appear in the Brightness/Contrast dialog box.

Ultimately, you can revert to the original, uncorrected image by either hiding or deleting the adjustment layers.

Applying an adjustment layer to a limited area

Although the adjustment layers do a fine job of bringing out the colors and details of the dark original, the orange-colored blossoms are now so vivid that they border on the garish. You'll see how you can compensate for this by adding a new adjustment layer that addresses color rather than lighting.

1 In the toolbox, select the Magic Wand tool ( ). In the tool options bar, type **48** for Tolerance, and make sure that New Selection ( ) and Contiguous are selected.

2 Click one of the two extremely bright blossoms in the upper area of the image. A selection marquee appears around most of the flower.

3 In the tool options bar, select Add To Selection ( ).

4 Click the second bright blossom to add it to the selection. If necessary, click again to add any unselected patches of color within the two blossom areas.

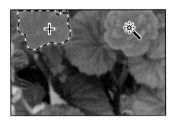 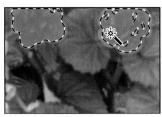 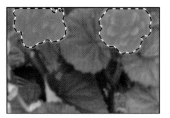

5 Choose Layer > New Adjustment Layer > Hue/Saturation. Click OK to accept the default name, Hue/Saturation 1. (You'll notice that the selection marquee disappears in the image window, but don't worry, because it's already done its job.)

6 Leave the Hue setting unchanged, but drag the Saturation slider to -20 and the Lightness setting to +5. Adjust the sliders again, if needed, and then click OK.

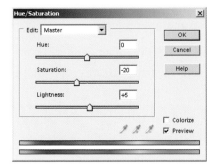

Notice that the changes affect only the two selected blossoms, not the rest of the picture.

7 Choose File > Save. In the Save As dialog box, save the file in the Lessons\My CIB Work folder, and name the file **04_02_Work.psd**, accepting Photoshop (PSD) as the Format. If Save In Version Set With Original is selected, be sure to deselect it before you click Save.

Even at its best, you probably wouldn't choose to hang this picture in your living room. But it does demonstrate both the flexibility and the dramatic improvements you can apply and use with Photoshop Elements 3.0.

💡 *For complex selections, you can use keyboard shortcuts with selection tools instead of tool options bar icons to temporarily switch between New, Add, or Subtract selection modes. Hold down Shift to add or Alt to subtract as you click or drag the selection tool.*

Comparing results of adjustment layers and auto fixes

You're almost finished with this project.

1 Using the File Browser, open the Autofix_04_03.jpg file in the Lessons\My CIB Work folder. Then close the File Browser.

This is one of the files you fixed by applying the Auto Fix options at the beginning of the lesson. (See "Getting started" on page 138 if you have not done that procedure.)

2 Choose Window > Images > Tile to arrange the files in the work area.

3 Examine each image and decide which one you prefer.

4 Choose File > Close All.

Congratulations, you've successfully completed another project.

In this project, you've experienced the power and versatility of adjustment layers. You've learned how to alter lighting and color settings in a way that is 100% reversible, even after you save and close the PSD file.

Project 4: Correcting parts of an image

Whether or not you make color and lighting adjustment directly or use adjustment layers, it doesn't always work to apply those changes to the entire image. Some pictures have combinations of problems that demand individual and separate attention.

Earlier in this lesson, you worked on an underexposed photograph of a little girl and a faded sepia-toned photograph of a little boy. You'll apply those same remedies to the different areas of another image, which has a combination of exposure problems. You'll intensify the over-bright tree branches and sky, and then draw out the details and colors for the shadowed pillar and wall.

Creating a rough selection

In this task, you'll select the area on the right side of the pillar where you see the leafy branches and sky. You'll begin by making a rough, rectangular selection of most of the area and then adding details to that selection.

Before you begin, make sure that you have enough time (10 or 15 minutes) to do both this procedure and the next one before you take a break, because the next task will refine the selection you make here.

1 Using the File Browser or Organizer, open the 04_04.jpg file, which is in the Lesson04 folder and is tagged with both the Lesson 4 and Project 4 tags.

2 In the toolbox, select the Rectangular Marquee tool (⬚), which is grouped with the Elliptical Marquee tool in the toolbox.

3 Drag from the upper right corner to the bottom of the image, to the right of the pillar. Make sure that the selection rectangle fits snugly against the right side of the image.

4 Select the Magnetic Lasso tool (⬡), which is grouped with the Lasso tool (◯) in the toolbox.

5 In the tool options bar, select Add To Selection (▢), *not* New Selection.

Review the other settings in the tool options bar, which should be Feather at 0 px, Width at 10 px, Edge Contrast at 10%, and Frequency at 57.

6 Click at the upper right corner of the selection rectangle to set an anchor point. Then move the Magnetic Lasso pointer across to the pillar and down its right edge. (You can just slide the pointer; it is not necessary to drag.)

7 When you reach the bottom, click once. Move the pointer inside the lower left corner of the original selection rectangle. Double-click to complete the selection, or drag the pointer to the starting point and click once to close the selection.

The Magnetic Lasso tool detects the edges of contrasting areas automatically but not perfectly. Go directly to the next procedure without deselecting.

Refining and saving the selection

The Magnetic Lasso tool does an excellent job of selecting areas that contrast sharply with the surrounding area. For this image, the leaves in some areas are similar enough to the values in the pillar that you may need to do some clean-up work.

1 Select the Zoom tool (🔍) in the toolbox and then Zoom In (🔍) in the tool options bar. Zoom in so that you can see details of the selection you made in the previous procedure.

(If the selection is no longer active, repeat "Creating a rough selection" on page 157.)

2 Scroll up and down the right side of the image, looking for areas where the selection marquee does not line up with the edge of the pillar.

3 Select the Polygonal Lasso tool (⌘).

4 Remove any areas of the pillar that are included in the selection, as follows:

• Select Subtract From Selection (⌘) in the tool options bar.

• Click once to set a starting anchor point.

• Move the Polygonal Lasso tool a short distance along the edge of the pillar, and click again as needed to set additional anchor points.

• Double-click the tool to close the shape and complete the selection removal. Or, move the tool close to the starting point until a small circle appears with the lasso pointer, and click to close the shape.

Note: If moving the pointer continues to create a line in the image window, then the selection is not closed. Try clicking the starting point of the selection or double-clicking again to close it.

5 Add any areas of the trees that the selection missed, as follows:

• Select Add To Selection (⌘) in the tool options bar.

• Click to set anchor points around the area that you want to add to the selection, and then close the selection.

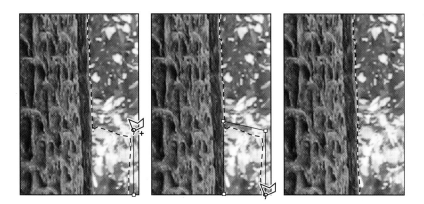

6 Choose Select > Save Selection.

7 In the Save Selection dialog box, type **Trees & Sky** to name the selection, and click OK.

Correcting an overexposed area of the image

One of the aims in this project is to intensify the color and contrast in the overexposed area where the trees and sky are. But you don't want to do that to the pillar and shaded area, which are already a bit darker than ideal. Your approach here is to divide and conquer—to apply different solutions to different areas of the image. Creating a copy of just the area you just selected is the first step of this process.

1 In the Layers palette, click More in the upper right corner of the Layers palette to open the Layers palette menu, and choose Palette Options.

2 Select the medium-sized thumbnail option, if it is not already selected, and click OK.

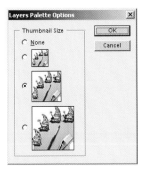

It's OK to select another size, but do not select None. The layer thumbnail can help you visualize what's happening at the layer level of this project.

3 Zoom out so that you can see the entire image, and then do one of the following:

• If the selection you made in the previous topic is still active, go immediately to Step 4.

• If the selection is not active, choose Select > Load Selection. Make sure that Trees & Sky is selected, and click OK.

4 Choose Edit > Copy (or press Ctrl + C) to copy the selected area.

5 Choose Edit > Paste (or press Ctrl + V) to paste the copied area onto a new layer, Layer 1.

In the image window, the only difference you'll see is that the selection marquee has disappeared. But in the Layers palette, you can see that there's a new layer.

6 With Layer 1 (the copy of the tree and sky area) selected in the Layers palette, set the blending mode to Multiply.

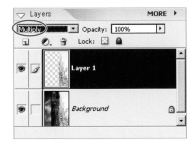

Now the trees and sky look more colorful.

Correcting an underexposed area with other blending modes

You can lighten the shadows of just the shaded areas with techniques that are similar—but different—from the ones you used to intensify the trees and sky.

1 In the Layers palette, select the Background layer.

2 Choose Select > Reselect, and then Select > Inverse.

Now the pillar and stucco wall are selected instead of the trees and sky.

Note: If you get a different selection or if the Reselect command is not available, choose Select > Load Selection, and then select the Invert option and Trees & Sky.

3 Choose Edit > Copy and then Edit > Paste.

Note: If an error message appears saying that the selected area is empty, make sure that the Background layer is selected in the Layers palette, and try again.

4 With Layer 2 (the copy of the pillar and wall area) selected in the Layers palette, choose Screen as the blending mode.

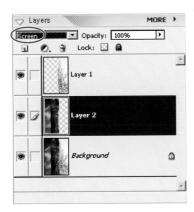

Adding more intensity and saving

Now the entire photograph looks much more lively. All that remains is to make any minor adjustments you like, and then see how this file compares to the one you automatically corrected at the beginning of this lesson.

1 Drag Layer 1 to New Layer ( ) in the Layers palette to create a duplicate layer, Layer 1 Copy.

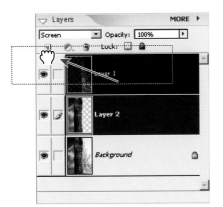

2 Drag Layer 2 to New Layer (⬛) in the Layers palette to create a duplicate layer, Layer 2 Copy.

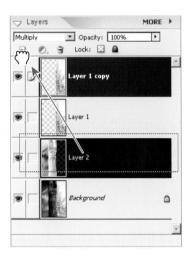

3 With Layer 2 Copy selected in the Layers palette, do the following:

• Choose Overlay as the blending mode.

• Click the arrow by Opacity to open the slider, and drag to 50%. Or type **50%**.

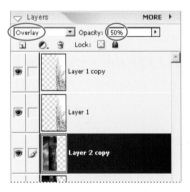

4 Examine the entire image, looking critically at the brightness and intensities in the different areas. Using your own judgment, adjust the opacity of the copied layers as needed to achieve the right balance in the image.

Note: You cannot change the Opacity or position of the Background layer, which is locked and protected by default.

5 When you are satisfied with the results, choose File > Save.

6 In the Save As dialog box, save the file in the Lessons\My CIB Work folder, naming the file **04_04_Work** and accepting Photoshop (PSD) as the Format. If Save In Version Set With Original is selected, be sure to deselect it before you click Save.

7 Leave the file open and go on to the next procedure.

Comparing your results to the auto-fixed version

Let's see how your careful work compares to the version you created earlier in this project.

1 Choose File > Browse Folders to open the File Browser.

2 Using the Folders palette, locate and select the My CIB Work folder in the Lessons folder.

3 Double-click the thumbnail of the Autofix_04_04.jpg file to open it.

If the 04_04.psd file is not still open from the previous procedure, double-click that thumbnail (in the same My CIB Work folder) to open it, too.

4 Close or minimize the File Browser.

5 Arrange the files side by side, using Window > Images > Tile, or by dragging and resizing them yourself.

6 When you finish comparing the two results, choose File > Close All.

Great news: You've finished the final project in this lesson. In this project, you've learned how to use selections with the other techniques you've practiced in Lesson 4 projects to correct images with complex exposure problems.

Saving and organizing your finished files

If you've already finished Lessons 2 and 3 in this book, you are familiar with this final phase of the lesson. You're going to add tags to the work files, which were already added to Organizer when you saved them, thanks to the Include In Organizer option in the Save As dialog box.

1 Click Photo Browser (⌷) on the Photoshop Elements Editor shortcuts bar to switch to Organizer. If Back To All Photos appears on the Organizer shortcuts bar, select it.

2 Choose File > Get Photos > From Files And Folders. Go to the My CIB Work folder, and select the four autofixed files that you prepared at the beginning of Lesson 4 (Autofix_04_01.jpg through Autofix_04_04.jpg.) Then click Get Photos.

3 Choose Find > Untagged Items.

4 Choose Edit > Select All or press Ctrl + A to select all the thumbnails, and then drag first the Lesson 4 and then the Work Files tags from the Tags palette to any one of the thumbnails to tag them all.

Note: If the Work Files tag doesn't appear in your Tags palette, see "Organizing your finished project files" on page 96 for instructions on how to create it.

5 Click and then Ctrl-click to select all five versions of the Project 2 file (the sepia-toned image of the little boy).

6 Choose Edit > Stack > Stack Selected Photos to organize the five versions under one thumbnail.

7 Repeat Steps 5 and 6 for the various versions of the other three projects.

You can now select Back To All Photos to see the entire catalog of thumbnails.

Congratulations to you again. You've now finished Lesson 4. In this lesson, you've used a variety of methods for rescuing images with exposure problems. You've used automatic fixes, layers with blending modes, adjustment layers, and a series of methods from the Enhance menu.

Review questions

1 Describe two ways to create an exact copy of an existing layer.

2 Where can you find the controls for adjusting the lighting in a photograph?

3 How do you change the arrangement of image windows in the work area?

4 What is an adjustment layer, and what are its unique benefits?

Review answers

1 Photoshop Elements 3.0 must be running in Standard Edit mode for either of these procedures. One method is to select the layer you want to duplicate in the Layers palette, and then choose Layer > Duplicate Layer. The other method is to drag the layer (placing the pointer on either the layer thumbnail or the layer name) to the New Layer button (⊡) in the Layers palette. In either case, you get two identical layers, stacked one above the other.

2 You can adjust the lighting for a photo in either Standard Edit or Quick Fix mode. In Standard Edit, you must use the Enhance > Adjust Lighting menu to open various dialog boxes that contain the controls. Or, you can choose Enhance > Auto Levels or Enhance > Auto Contrast. In Quick Fix mode, you can use the Lighting palette in the Palette Bin.

3 You cannot rearrange image windows in Quick Fix, which displays only one photograph at a time. In Standard Edit, there are several ways you can arrange them. One is to choose Window > Images, and choose one of the items listed there. Another method is to use the buttons in the upper right corner of the work area, just below the Minimize, Restore/Maximize, and Close buttons for Photoshop Elements 3.0. A third way is to drag the image window title bar to move an image window and to drag a corner to resize it (provided Maximize mode is not currently active).

4 An adjustment layer does not contain an image; instead, it modifies some quality of all the layers below it in the Layer palette. For example, a Brightness/Contrast layer can alter the brightness and contrast of any underlying layers. One advantage of using an adjustment layer instead of adjusting an existing layer directly is that it is easily reversible. You can click the eye icon for the adjustment layer to remove the effects instantly, and then restore the eye icon to apply the adjustments again. You can change a setting in the adjustment layer to zero to reset that option to its original condition.

5 | Using Photos in Other Forms

You can keep images in all kinds of forms: as on-screen image files, photo prints, in other types of documents, or as video, DVDs, and web pages, to name a few. Photoshop Elements 3.0 makes it possible for you to convert images from one media to another without straining your brain.

In this lesson, you will learn how to do the following:

- Import images from PDF documents.

- Import individual frames from video clips as still images.

- Fix interlacing problems from captured video frames.

- Create panorama views from a series of individual photographs.

- Create a multi-page album of favorite photographs.

- Print a contact sheet for all or part of an Organizer catalog.

Most people can complete all the work in this lesson in an hour or less. The lesson includes five independent projects, so you can do them all at once or in different work sessions. All the projects in this lesson are relatively short. Some can be completed in about five minutes; others can take a little longer, depending on the amount of time you spend exploring alternate choices available for that project.

If you are starting your work in this book at Lesson 5, make sure that you have already copied the project files from the CD attached to the inside back cover of this book. See "Copying the Classroom in a Book files" on page 3.

Getting started

In Lesson 1, you used Organizer to add photos to your catalog. In this lesson, you'll use Editor to import images from other formats. You'll also use Editor to stitch together various photographs to create a panorama. The last two projects in this lesson use Organizer to create output images in different ways.

1 Start Photoshop Elements 3.0 in Standard Edit mode.

2 (Optional) You can hide the Palette Bin (by clicking the arrow below it or choosing Window > Palette Bin) because you won't need it for this lesson.

You can start with any project in this lesson, but if you start with Project 4 or Project 5, you must switch to Organizer.

Project 1: Importing images from a PDF document

If you have some experience using the Internet, you're undoubtedly familiar with Adobe Reader files, PDF (Portable Document Format) files. This is an efficient and relatively secure way to share complex documents on the web or on a local network.

You can import images from a PDF document for use in Photoshop Elements. You'll see how when you do these easy steps.

1 In Standard Edit, choose File > Import > PDF Image.

2 In the Look In pop-up menu of the Select PDF For Image Import dialog box, find and open the Lesson05 folder in the Lessons folder.

3 Select the 05_01.pdf file, and click Open.

4 In the PDF Image Import dialog box, do one of the following:

• Select one of the images to import, and click OK.

• Select a few images to import by holding down Ctrl and clicking the thumbnails. Then click OK.

• Press Ctrl + A to select all eight images, and click OK.

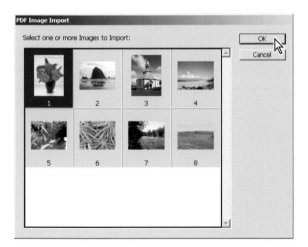

The pictures you selected open in individual image windows.

5 Choose File > Save, and save the file in the My CIB Work folder in the Lessons folder, using the file name that appears automatically. If Save In Version Set With Original is selected, be sure to deselect it before you click Save. Then close the file.

6 Repeat Step 5 for any other images you imported from the PDF file.

Note: Some PDF documents include security features that prevent unauthorized readers from using the files. You cannot import images from those documents without the appropriate permissions or passwords.

Project 2: Importing still images from video

If you have videos that you can view on your computer, you can capture individual frames of that movie and use them as still images.

In this example, the video shows high-speed action. The video process interlaces images, so that an ordinary capture grabs two frames and shows alternating screen lines of each one. Interlacing becomes more obvious when the images are fast-moving. Photoshop Elements 3.0 has a built-in feature for correcting this problem.

1 In Standard Edit, choose File > Import > Frame From Video.

2 In the Frame From Video dialog box, click Browse.

3 In the Open dialog box, open the Lesson05 folder in the Lessons folder, select the 05_02.avi file, and click Open.

4 Click Play (▶) to review the video. Then drag the slider under the image until you find a frame you want to save as a still image.

💡 *You can press the left and right arrow keys on your keyboard to advance or reverse frame-by-frame.*

5 Click Grab Frame, and then click Done.

The saved frame appears in an image window, but the result looks like a double-exposure.

6 Choose Filter > Video > De-Interlace.

7 In the De-Interlace dialog box, click OK.

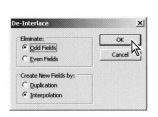 

The image clears up.

8 Choose File > Save As, and save the file in the My CIB Work folder, naming it **05_02_Work**, and accepting Photoshop (PSD) for Format. If Save In Version Set With Original is selected, be sure to deselect it before you click Save. Then close the file (choose File > Close) because you've finished this project.

Project 3: Merging photos into a panorama

The four photos you'll use for this project are incremental views of a river running through farmland. This is an ideal opportunity for learning how to create panoramas because of the strong, distinctive lines made by roads running between the fields. You'll use those roads as a guide for perfecting the orientation and placement of the photos, but only after Photoshop Elements does most of the work for you.

1 In Standard Edit, choose File > New > Photomerge® Panorama.

2 Click Browse in the dialog box that opens. Go to the Lessons\Lesson05 folder, select the 05_03a, 05_03b, 05_03c, and 05_03d files, and click Open.

3 If any other files appear under Source Files in the dialog box, select them and click Remove. (For this project, the photomerge works best if the files are in alphabetical order.) Then click OK.

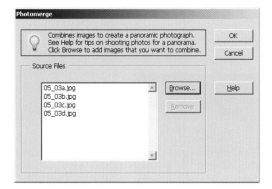

Note: You can also start the photomerge process in Organizer. Find and select the thumbnails of the individual photographs that make up the panorama and select them. Then choose File > New > Photomerge Panorama in Editor. Photoshop Elements automatically switches to Standard Edit.

Wait while Photoshop Elements opens and closes windows to create the panorama. If a message appears telling you that some images could not be automatically arranged, follow the instructions for arranging them manually.

4 In the large Photomerge dialog box, do the following to fine-tune the panorama:

• Using the Select Image tool ( ), select the second photo from the left.

• Select the Rotate Image tool ( ), and drag counter-clockwise to rotate the second photo, so that the road in the distance is parallel with its position in the picture to the right.

Note: It may help to click the Snap To Image check box to deselect it and to zoom in, using the Zoom tool ( ) in the upper left side of the dialog box.

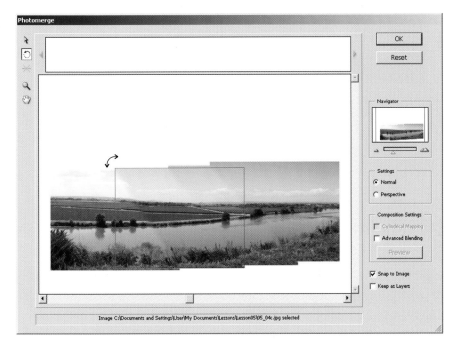

• Switch back to the Select Image tool and drag the second picture down slightly so that the roads in the two center pictures line up perfectly. (As you drag the image, its appearance becomes semi-transparent so that you see the underlying area of the third photograph.)

• Repeat the process for the picture on the far left so that the road lines up with the road visible in the second picture.

• When you are satisfied with the results, select Advanced Blending, and then click
Preview.

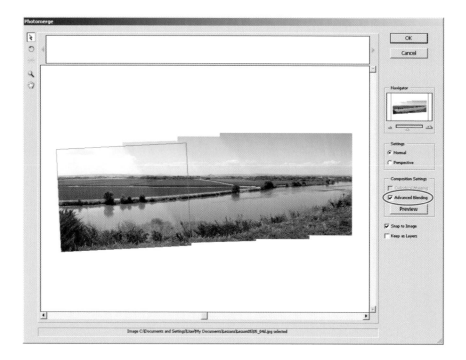

5 After examining the preview, click Exit Preview. Then click OK.

The Photomerge dialog box closes, and Photoshop Elements goes to work. You'll see
windows open and close as you wait for Editor to create the panorama.

6 Select the Crop tool (⊐) and drag a cropping selection around the image, being careful
not to include any of the checkerboard areas where the image is transparent. Then click
Commit (✔) in the tool options bar to crop the image.

7 Choose File > Save, and save the image in the My CIB Work folder as **05_03_Work**, and select JPEG as the Format. If Save In Version Set With Original is selected, be sure to deselect it before you click Save. After you click Save, the JPEG Options dialog box appears. For Quality, select 12, Maximum, and click OK.

Note: *The original work file, called Untitled-1, remains open. Close it now, and do not save the changes.*

Extra-credit exercise

If you want to try something different, repeat the panorama procedure up to Step 3. Then, instead of moving and rotating the images to get the roads aligned, select Perspective in the Photomerge dialog box. Then select the Vanishing Point tool ( ) and click near the far right side of the image, just above the horizon. Don't forget to select Advanced Blending before you click OK.

Panorama perspective with reset vanishing point, and cropped version of the same image

Project 4: Creating an album for on-screen viewing

Creations are forms in which you can save, share, and present selected images from your Organizer catalog. You can save Creations in several ways: to share online, as a slide show with audio, or by printing. The process is almost foolproof, and the choices are fun.

In this project, you'll create a sample album for on-screen viewing in PDF format.

1 In Photoshop Elements 3.0 Editor, click Photo Browser ( ) in the shortcuts bar to switch to Organizer.

2 In Organizer, choose File > New > Photo Album Pages to load the Create Photo Album Pages wizard.

3 On Step 1: Creation Set-up, do the following:

• On the right side of the dialog box, select No Borders, if it is not already selected.

• In the lower left area of the dialog box, make sure that Title Page, Captions, and Page Numbers are selected, or select them now.

• In the Photos Per Page pop-up menu, select Sequence: 1, 2 Repeat.

• Click Next Step.

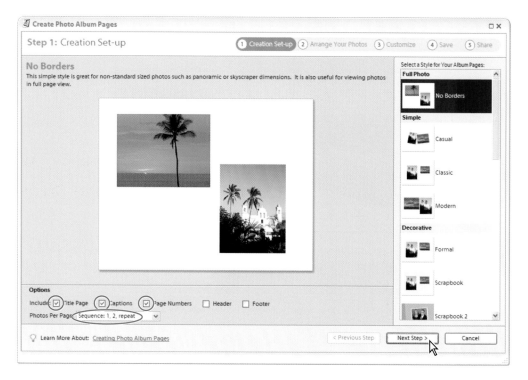

4 On Step 2: Arrange Your Photos, click Add Photos to open the Add Photos dialog box, and do the following:

• Select Tag and use the pop-up menu to choose Lesson 5.

• Click Add Photos. In the Add Photos dialog box, select check boxes for at least four or five images that you want to include. Click OK.

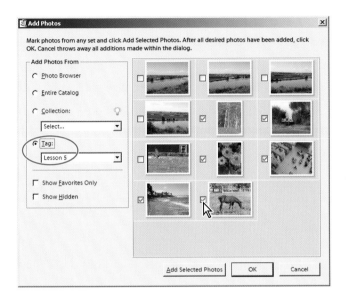

If a message about resolution appears, click OK in the message window to close it.

• Drag the thumbnails to rearrange them in the order you want to use. (The first image will appear on the title page of your album.)

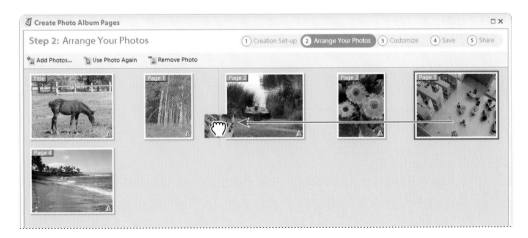

• If you want to add other photos or remove a selected image from the album pages, use the Add Photos and Remove Photo buttons above the thumbnail display.

5 Click Next Step to go to Step 3: Customize, and do the following:

• Double-click the placeholder text. Type **My Sample Album** in the Title dialog box, and click Done. (You can change the font settings first, if you want other options.)

• Drag the image to move it, or drag the corners of the marquee around the image to resize it.

• Drag the Title text box to move it, or drag the corners to resize the text box. (This does not resize the text.)

• Either click the arrow (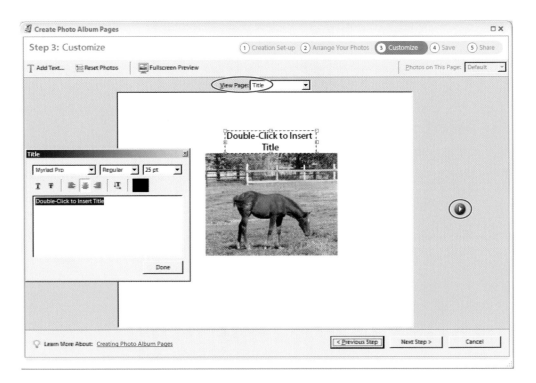) or use the View Page pop-up menu to go to the next page of the album.

• Repeat the tasks you just did for the Title page (moving and resizing the image, adding text, and advancing to the next page) for each of the remaining pages in the album.

Note: If there is already a caption embedded in the file, that caption will appear on the page. You can either edit the caption or leave it as it is.

• When you have customized all the pages, click Next Step.

6 On Step 4: Save, type **05_04_Work** for Album Pages Name, or select Use Title For Name. Then click Save.

7 On Step 5: Share, select Create A PDF. Then do the following:

• Select Optimize For Viewing Onscreen (if it is not already selected) in the Save As PDF dialog box, and click OK.

• Save the file in the My CIB Work folder you created in the Lessons folder, and click Save.

When Photoshop Elements finishes generating the PDF file, you'll be invited to view it. If you accept, Adobe Reader will automatically open the file. Use the arrow keys on your keyboard or the arrows at the top of the Adobe Reader viewing area to turn the pages.

8 Click Done to close the Create Photo Album Pages wizard.

Note: If you do not have Adobe Reader (or an earlier version, called Adobe Acrobat Reader) installed on your computer, you can install a copy from the Adobe Photoshop Elements 3.0 application CD or download a free copy of the latest version from the Adobe website (www.adobe.com).

If you look at the file size of the My Sample Album.pdf (right-click the file in Windows Explorer and choose Properties), you'll see that it is still relatively small. Typically, an album PDF file is smaller than the sum of the file sizes for all the individual pictures in it. This makes it not only an attractive way to view and present your favorite photos, but also an efficient way to share them through e-mail. (See "E-mailing photos" on page 28.)

About other Creations

There are many other creative ways to store and share your favorite photographs. Click Create ( ) on the Organizer shortcuts bar (or choose File > New > Creation) to open the Creation Setup window. Look here for examples and explanations about the possibilities for photo presentations and other formats ideal for sharing pictures.

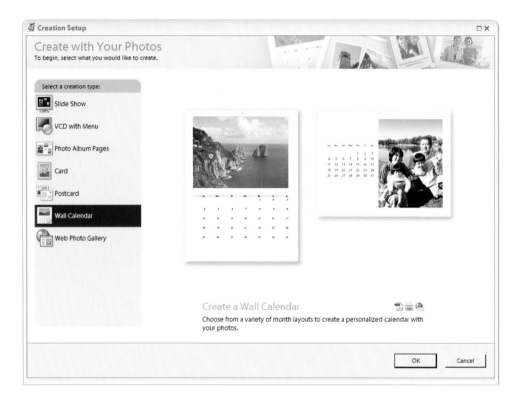

Project 5: Printing a contact sheet

Here's a popular feature that helps you identify images in a catalog. A printed contact sheet can be a great time saver when you store your images on CDs, helping you identify in a glance which pictures you've stored on the CD.

1 In Organizer, select the Find boxes for the Lesson 5 and Project 5 tags. (The thumbnails that appear are the same six images tagged for Project 4 in this lesson.)

2 Choose Edit > Select All, and then choose File > Print.

3 In the Print Photos dialog box, do the following:

• For (1) Select Printer, select an available printer.

• For (2) Select Type Of Print, choose Contact Sheet from the pop-up menu.

• For (3) Select A Layout, type or click the arrows to change the number of thumbnails per row. Then, under Add A Text Label, select the items you want to appear below each thumbnail.

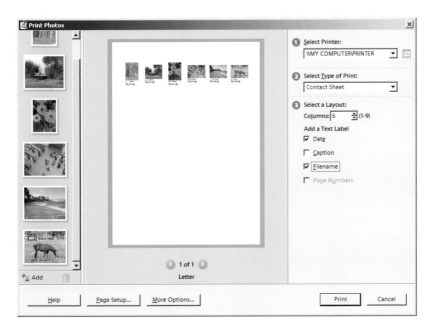

4 (Optional) Do either or both of the following:

• In the lower left area of the Print Photos dialog box, click Add. Select the Entire
Catalog option, and then select more images to add to your contact sheet. Click OK to
close the Add Photos dialog box.

• Select a thumbnail on the left side of the Print Photos dialog box for a picture you want
to exclude, and then click Remove Selected Items (🗑) to remove that image from the
contact sheet.

*Note: If you want to change the paper size, click Page Setup and use the Paper Size
options.*

5 When you are finished, do one of the following:

• Click Print.

• Click Cancel to close the dialog box without printing.

Saving and organizing your finished files

If you've already finished earlier lessons in this book, you are familiar with this final
phase of the lesson. You're going to add tags to the work files, which were already added
to Organizer when you saved them, thanks to the Include In Organizer option in the Save
As dialog box.

1 If Back To All Photos appears above the thumbnails area, select it.

2 Choose Find > Untagged Items.

3 Choose Edit > Select All or press Ctrl + A to select all the thumbnails.

4 Drag the Work Files tag and then the Lesson 5 tag to the thumbnails to apply them.

You can now select Back To All Photos to see the entire catalog of thumbnails.

*Note: If you hid the Palette Bin at the beginning of this lesson, switch to Editor and click
the Open Palette Bin arrow in the lower right corner of the work area to reopen it so that
you're set up correctly for the next projects.*

Congratulations! You've now finished Lesson 5. In this lesson, you've learned how to
extract images from PDF files and videos and import them into Photoshop Elements.
You've created panoramas, photo albums, and contact sheets. In the process, you've seen
how Editor and Organizer share responsibilities for different tasks.

Review questions

1 How are the methods you used to import new images in this lesson different from the techniques you used in Lesson 1?

2 How do you fix what looks like a double exposure in an imported video-frame image?

3 Which component of Photoshop Elements 3.0 can align separate photos into a panorama view? How do you start the process?

4 How do you turn your photographs into slide shows, calendars, photo albums, web galleries, and other forms that are ideal for sharing with others?

Review answers

1 In Lesson 1, you gathered existing image files into Organizer. In this lesson, you used the Import command, which is available only in Editor. You used that command to import selected images from a PDF file and a video clip. One of the things you can do (but did not in this lesson), is to gather all the photos from a PDF file into an Organizer catalog. If you want to try this, choose File > Get Photos > From Files And Folders, and then select PDF Files from the Files Of Type pop-up menu at the bottom of the Get Photos From Files And Folders dialog box.

2 You can choose Filter > Video > De-Interlace to fix the video import.

3 You use Photoshop Elements 3.0 Editor in Standard Edit mode to create panoramas. Choose File > New > Photomerge Panorama to start the process. It's not even necessary to open the files before you begin merging. However, you can also start a photomerge in Organizer by selecting the thumbnails of the images that will make up the panorama and then choosing File > New > Photomerge Panorama in Editor.

4 You choose File > New > Creation to start the process of preparing photos for presentations in various other formats. You can select from a variety of designer layouts and styles. For some types, such as PDF slide shows, you can include music files, narration, and transition effects.

6 | Repairing, Retouching, and Replacing Flaws

Some pictures have all the elements you want—good color, proper exposure, good composition—but there's a problem with the subject. It could be a flaw in the skin, a tear in the photograph, or the wrong kind of weather. Photoshop Elements 3.0 puts tools at your fingertips for correcting all these and more.

In this lesson you will do the following:

- Use blending modes and opacity changes to make layers interact.

- Make selections using various tools in various modes.

- Refine active selections and edit saved selections.

- Use the Styles And Effects palette to apply simulated weather conditions.

- Use the Eyedropper and Gradient tools to draw a realistic-looking sky.

- Crop panorama files.

- Retouch and remove wrinkles and skin flaws.

- Use the Dodge tool to underexpose a limited area of the image.

- Work with a mask.

- Use the Clone Stamp tool to repair missing areas.

Most people can complete all the work in this lesson in an hour and a half or less. The lesson includes eight, independent projects, so you can do them all at once or in different work sessions. The projects vary in length and complexity. Some can be completed in less than five minutes; others can take 20 minutes or more, depending on how meticulous you are with your work.

Before you begin, make sure that you have accurately copied the project files from the CD attached to the inside back cover of this book. See "Copying the Classroom in a Book files" on page 3. Although you can do this lesson out of order, it requires some file structures, custom tags, and skills covered in Lessons 1 and 2.

Getting started

The first six projects in this lesson demonstrate different ways to create artificial sky conditions in photographs—how to "change the weather." Each of these six procedures is relatively easy and short. In the process of exploring ways to alter the skies, you'll use four different photographs. Sometimes you'll create realistic-looking skies. Sometimes, your results may be decidedly stylized, depending on the choices you make.

The last two projects in this lesson show you how to remove wrinkles, spots, blemishes, tears, and other flaws from scanned images and digital photographs.

1 Start Photoshop Elements 3.0 in Standard Edit mode.

2 Open the Palette and Photo Bins, if they are not already open, by clicking the arrows
(▲) and (▮▸) at the bottom of the work area or by choosing Window > Palette Bin and
Window > Photo Bin to place check marks next to those commands.

3 Review the contents of the Palette Bin, making sure that the Layers, Navigator, Styles
And Effects, and Undo History palettes are there.

Note: For help with Palette Bin contents, see "Using the Palette Bin" on page 59.

You can start with almost any of the weather projects in this lesson, because most of them
are independent of each other in both subject matter and skill level. The exception is
Weather project 6, which uses a file copy that you create in Weather project 5.

Weather project 1: Making blue sky more intense

Both this first project and the next one use the same underlying photograph, showing a
building with curving roof lines. The building looks fine, but the sky is too pale. Fortunately, it's a simple thing to fix and uses a technique you've already encountered in earlier
lessons in this book.

1 Using either the File Browser or Organizer, find and open the 06_01.jpg file, which is
in the Lessons\Lesson06 folder and tagged for Lesson 6 and Project 1.

2 In the toolbox, select the Magic Wand tool (✎).

3 In the tool options bar, type **32** for Tolerance, and make sure that Contiguous is
selected.

4 Click in the middle of the sky area.

*Note: A single click should select the entire sky area. If you get different results, deselect
(Select > Deselect), and review the settings in the tool options bar before you try Step 4
again.*

5 Choose Edit > Copy and then Edit > Paste. Or, press Ctrl + C to copy and Ctrl + V to paste.

6 In the Layers palette, make sure the new layer (Layer 1) is selected, and choose Multiply as the blending mode.

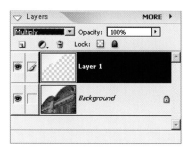

7 Choose File > Save, and save the results as **06_01_Work** using Photoshop (PSD) as the Format. Choose the My CIB Work folder you created in the Lessons folder as the location. If Save In Version Set With Original is selected, be sure to deselect it before you click Save.

You can close the file now because you're finished with this project.

Refining a Magic Wand selection

If you have trouble getting a perfect selection with the Magic Wand tool, you have lots of methods to improve it.

• *Start over (Select > Deselect), and click a slightly different spot in the area you're attempting to select. Your original click may have sampled pixels that are on one extreme or the other of the color variations you are trying to select.*

• *Adjust the Tolerance setting in the tool options bar either up (to include more colors and a larger area) or down (to include fewer colors and a smaller area).*

• *Select Add To Selection ( ) or Subtract From Selection ( ) in the tool options bar, and click areas that you want to add or remove from the selection. Consider also adjusting the Tolerance at this point, if the additional clicks create other problems in the selection.*

• *Use another selection tool, such as a lasso tool or a marquee tool, with Add To Selection ( ) or Subtract From Selection ( ) active in the tool options bar.*

• *Use the Selection Brush tool ( ) to paint areas into the selection.*

Weather project 2: Staging a fake storm

For this project, you'll cause a dramatic shift in the weather. You'll borrow some storm clouds from another photograph, and then use a Layer Style to unleash precipitation on the scene.

You'll use the same start file as you used for the first project. Because you saved your results as a Photoshop (PSD) file, the original JPEG file is unchanged. You'll also need to open a photograph of the storm.

1 Using either the File Browser or Organizer, find and open both the 06_01.jpg file and the 06_Storm.jpg file, both of which are tagged for Lesson 6 and Project 2, and are stored in the Lessons\Lesson06 folder.

Note: *If one image fills the entire work area and cannot be resized, choose Window > Images > Maximize Mode to deselect that command, removing its check mark.*

2 With both image windows visible and the 06_01 image active, hold down Shift and drag the building Background layer into the storm image window.

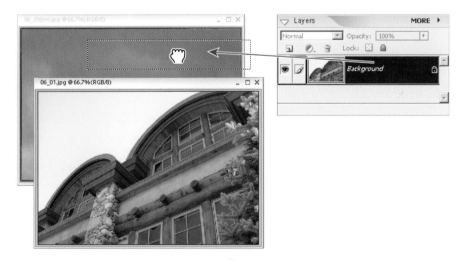

You can close the 06_01.jpg image now, without saving it.

3 Using the same options for the Magic Wand tool that you used in the previous procedure, select the sky.

4 Choose Edit > Delete (or press the Delete key) to erase the original pale blue sky so that the dark storm clouds show through in that area. Then choose Select > Deselect.

5 With Layer 1 selected, choose Layer > Merge Down to permanently combine the two layers.

6 In the Styles And Effects palette, choose Layer Styles and Image Effects in the pop-up menus, and then double-click the Rain thumbnail to apply that style.

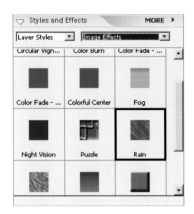

When a message appears, asking if you want to make the background a layer, click OK and then accept the default name, Layer 0.

7 Choose File > Save As, and save the finished file as **06_02_Work** in the My CIB Work folder you created in the Lessons folder. If Save In Version Set With Original is selected, be sure to deselect it before you click Save.

Congratulations, you've finished manipulating the weather for two versions of this photograph. You can now close any open files, and go on to the next project.

In these two projects, you've practiced making selections with the Magic Wand tool and applying a blending mode. You've copied a layer from one image into another image. You've done the sometimes essential job of converting the background into a layer by renaming it. You've also merged two layers so that Layer Styles, Effects, Filters, or other changes can be applied to both parts of the image equally.

About viewing modes and image window arrangements

When you work in Quick Fix mode, only one image file appears in the work area, regardless of how many files are open. The inactive, open files appear as thumbnails in the Photo Bin but not in the work area.

When you work in Standard Edit mode, other arrangements are possible. You can usually adjust the size and placement of image windows in the work area. If you can't arrange individual windows freely, then your view is probably Maximize Mode. If opening or closing some files causes unexpected rearrangements of image windows, your view is probably set to Automatically Tile.

Maximize *fills the work area with the active image window, so it's the only one you can see.*

Tile *automatically resizes and arranges all open images so that the image windows cover the work area. If Automatically Tile mode is active when you close an image file or open a new one, Photoshop Elements will rearrange the image windows in tile formation.*

Multi-window *enables you to resize, arrange, or minimize files.*

There are two ways to switch from one mode to another.

• Use the Window > Images menu and choose the arrangement you want: Maximize, Tile, or Cascade. Or, if there is a check mark on the Maximize command, choosing Maximize again deactivates it and switches to Multi-window mode.

• Select an icon on the far right end of the menu bar.

The available icons vary, depending on which viewing mode is active and on the size of the work area on your monitor. If the work area is reduced, these icons may not appear. The illustration below shows which icons you'll see in different modes.

Icons available with Maximize mode active, Automatically Tile mode active, and Multi-window mode active

For more information, see Adobe Photoshop Elements 3.0 Help (choose Help > Photoshop Elements Help).

Weather project 3: Clearing a cloudy sky

The subject photograph represents a common problem: It's your once-in-a-lifetime trip, and on the day you visit a world-famous landmark, the weather doesn't cooperate. Your picture looks dull, which curtails your bragging rights to friends and family.

In the sample picture you'll use for this project, the sky above the chateau holds almost no hint of blue, so using a blending mode to intensify it is no help. Instead, you'll use another photograph of cheerful blue skies and paste it into the chateau image. For a convincing touch of realism, you'll add a lens flare, as if the sun caught your camera.

Adding the sky from another image

For the ultimate in sky realism, use a real sky, as you did in Weather project 2. If you keep a collection of sky pictures, you can then select the type of sky you want to show, and paste it into your own pictures.

To safeguard the original image, you'll work on a copy of the Background layer.

1 Using either the File Browser or Organizer, find and open both the 06_03.jpg file and the 06_Blue.jpg file, both of which are tagged for Project 3 and are in the Lessons\Lesson06 folder.

2 With the 06_03 file active (the chateau) choose Layer > Duplicate Layer, and click OK to accept Background Copy as the layer name. Click the eye (👁) for the Background layer to hide it, leaving the Background Copy layer selected.

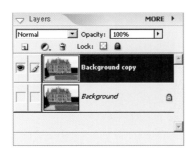

3 Select the Magic Wand tool (✎), make sure that 32 Tolerance and Contiguous are selected in the tool options bar, and then click once in the clouds to select the entire sky.

If the selection missed some areas of the sky, hold down Shift and click in those areas.

4 Press Delete (or choose Edit > Delete) to replace the sky area with the checkerboard pattern representing transparency. Then deselect (Select > Deselect or press Ctrl + D).

5 Move the image windows so that you can see both images.

Note: If one image fills the work area, choose Window > Images > Cascade.

6 Hold down Shift and drag the Background layer (sky) into the 06_03 (chateau) image.

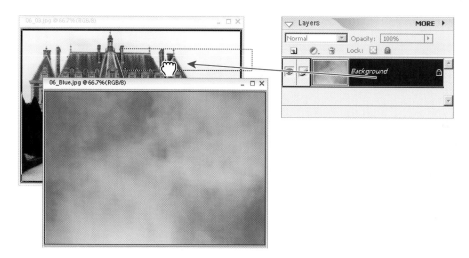

Holding down the Shift key automatically centers the layer in the second image. Close the 06_Blue.jpg file.

7 In the Layers palette, do the following:

• Drag the Background Copy layer above Layer 1.

• Leave Background Copy selected.

• Choose Layer > Merge down.

💡 *You can change the look of the pasted-in sky by selecting and transforming the sky layer. For example, use the Move tool (⬆️) to stretch the layer by dragging the corner anchor points. Or, position the Move tool pointer beyond a corner point until it changes to a curved double arrow, and rotate the layer. You can also choose Image > Rotate > Flip Layer Horizontal or Flip Layer Vertical to reverse it in one or two clicks.*

Creating a reflection of the sun

Here's an easy way to add a dramatic splash to your sky, whether artificial, pasted-in, or original to the photograph. You'll save the results as a separate version of the image.

1 Choose File > Save, and save the layered chateau image file as **06_03_Work.psd** in your My CIB Work folder in the Lessons folder. If Save In Version Set With Original is selected, be sure to deselect it before you click Save.

Before you continue, make sure that Layer 1 (the merged blue sky and chateau) is still selected in the Layers palette.

2 In the Styles And Effects palette, choose Filters on the left pop-up menu and Render on the right pop-up menu.

3 Double-click the thumbnail for the Lens Flare filter.

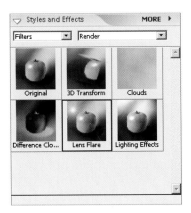

4 In the Lens Flare dialog box, drag the crosshairs to position the primary lens flare somewhere in the sky area.

(We liked a position low in the sky, close to the horizon so that it looks as if the sun is almost behind the chateau.)

5 Make the lens flare more subtle by dragging the Brightness slider to the left to reduce the value to about 90% and by selecting 35mm Prime. Then click OK.

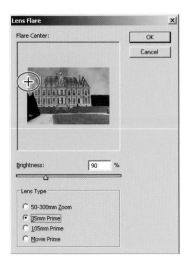

6 Choose File > Save As, and name this version of the image **06_03b_Work.psd**, being careful to include the *b* in the file name. (The file should already be located in the My CIB Work folder and in Photoshop (PSD) Format.) If Save In Version Set With Original is selected, be sure to deselect it before you click Save. Then close the file.

Good job! You've completed another project.

Weather project 4: Applying weather-like styling

In this quick project, you'll make snowflakes flood from the sky.

1 Using either the File Browser or Organizer, find and open the 06_04.jpg file, which is tagged for Lesson 6 and Project 4, and is in the Lessons\Lesson06 folder.

2 In the Styles And Effects palette, do the following:

• Choose Effects and Image Effects in the two pop-up menus.

• Double-click the Blizzard thumbnail to apply that effect to the image.

The Effect itself appears on a new layer, Background Copy.

3 Select the Background layer in the Layers palette.

4 In the Styles And Effects palette, choose Layer Styles and Image Effects, and then double-click the Snow thumbnail to apply a different type and texture of snow to the image.

When a message appears, asking if you want to make the background a layer, click OK and then accept the default name, Layer 0.

5 (Optional) To create near white-out conditions, drag the Background Copy layer to the New Layer icon in the Layers palette (or choose Layer > Duplicate Layer).

6 Choose File > Save As, and save the file in the My CIB Work folder you created in the Lessons folder, naming the file **06_04_Work.psd** and saving it with Photoshop (PSD) as its Format. Be sure to deselect Save In Version Set With Original if it is selected.

7 Close the file.

Congratulations, you've finished another one. In this project, you've seen how easy it is to apply some Effects and Filters that simulate weather conditions.

Weather project 5: Using a gradient fill

The subject photograph for this project is an uncropped panorama, similar to the one you created in Lesson 5. The panorama was created by matching the overlapping areas of six different photographs of a mountain range. Although the Advanced Blending option in the Panorama dialog box did a good job of blending the valley and mountains of this panorama, you can still see the seams in the sky.

One way to fix that is to substitute a blue gradient for the real sky.

Creating and saving a sky selection

Your first task is to protect the mountains and valley from the changes you'll apply. That means selecting only the sky area, so that only it changes.

At the end of this procedure, you're going to save two work copies of the file: one for this project (Weather project 5) and a duplicate that you'll use in the next section (for Weather project 6).

1 Using either the File Browser or Organizer, find and open the 06_05.jpg file, which is in the Lessons\Lesson06 folder and tagged for Lesson 6 and Project 5.

2 Select the Magic Wand tool ( ). In the tool options bar, do the following:

• Select New Selection ( ).

• Type **48** for Tolerance.

• Select Contiguous

3 Click the Magic Wand in the middle of the sky.

Most of the sky is selected, but there are probably a few areas above and below the selection that were missed.

4 Select Add To Selection (📋) in the tool options bar. Then click the Magic Wand in each area the first selection click missed, including the two white areas above the sky on either side of the image.

5 Choose Select > Save Selection. Name the selection **Sky**, and click OK.

6 Choose File > Save As, and save it as **06_05_Work** in the My CIB Work folder you created earlier, making sure that Photoshop (PSD) appears in the Format option. If Save In Version Set With Original is selected, deselect it before you click Save.

7 Choose File > Duplicate, and type **06_06_Work** in the Duplicate Image dialog box when it appears. Then either close it (File > Close) or click the Minimize button (–) to set it aside for later, when you work on Weather project 6.

Weather project 6 requires the same selection as Weather project 5. By saving a duplicate of your Weather project 5 work file, the saved selection will be available so you won't have to do this job over.

Adding a gradient sky

The key to creating a realistic sky is to get the right colors. For this gradient, you'll use samples of real sky colors from the original photograph.

Before you begin, make sure that 06_05_Work.psd is open and is the active image. If the Sky selection is not in effect, load it now (Select > Reselect, or Select > Load Selection).

1 In the toolbox, select the Eyedropper tool (🖋).

2 Click the deepest blue in the sky, close to the top of the merged images. The deep blue color appears as the Foreground Color swatch in the toolbox.

3 In the toolbox, click the Switch Foreground And Background Colors button (↳) so that the blue fills the Background Color swatch and white becomes the Foreground Color.

4 Click the lightest blue in the sky, close to the mountains.

The light blue color fills the Foreground Color swatch.

5 In the toolbox, select the Gradient tool (▬), and then select or verify the following settings in the tool options bar:

• Foreground To Background (the default). If this is not selected, click the arrow to open the Gradient Picker, select the Foreground To Background thumbnail, and then click anywhere outside the Gradient Picker to close it.

• Linear Gradient (▬).

- Normal as the Mode.
- 100% Opacity.

💡 *There are two ways to see the gradient names in the Gradient Picker: Let the pointer hover over a thumbnail until a tool tip appears, or click the arrow (▶) to open the palette menu and choose Text Only, Small List, or Large List.*

6 Drag the Gradient tool straight up from just above the mountains to just below the top of the sky area.

Note: If the gradient completely fills the image, choose Edit > Undo Gradient, and reload your saved Sky selection (Select > Load Selection) before you try again. However, if your gradient appears only in the sky area, but you want to try different starting and ending points for the gradient, simply drag the Gradient tool again. It is not necessary to undo the first gradient.

7 Choose Select > Deselect (or press Ctrl + D). Then save the file, but do not close it yet.

Note: If you wanted a sunset, use the radial gradient (▪) and select a warm pastel for the Foreground Color. Start the gradient near the horizon and drag up and away at an angle. Apply a Lens Flare at a strategic point near the center of the gradient.

You'll do one more procedure with this file at the end of the next project.

Weather project 6: Using a Filter as the sky

This is your final weather project in this lesson. In this case, you'll use the same panorama that you worked on in Weather project 5, but you'll use the copy you made.

Instead of adding a completely realistic sky, you'll apply a stylized texture to the sky area. Then you'll try different techniques to make the artificial sky as realistic as possible.

Adding the Filter

If you have just completed Weather project 5, the Foreground and Background Colors in the toolbox will still be a light blue and a dark blue. That's just what you want. If those colors are no longer selected, use the Eyedropper tool to select them again. (See Steps 1-4 in "Adding a gradient sky" on page 205.)

1 Select the 06_06_work thumbnail in the Photo Bin to open its image window. If the selection is still active, deselect it now (choose Select > Deselect or press Ctrl + D).

Or, if you closed that file, use the Folders palette in the File Browser to navigate to the Lessons\My CIB Work folder. Then select the 06_06_work.psd thumbnail and open the file.

Note: Although the file was added to your Organizer catalog when you saved it, dupli-cating the image file does not duplicate the Organizer tags. Therefore, using Organizer to find the file is not as efficient as for other project files that are already tagged.

2 In the Layers palette, click New Layer (▣) to create a new, blank layer, Layer 1. Leave Layer 1 selected.

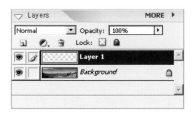

3 In the Styles And Effects palette, choose Filters and Render in the pop-up menus, and then double-click the Clouds thumbnail.

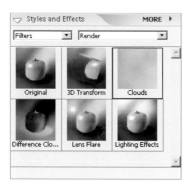

The cloud layer now covers the entire image. The current Foreground Color and Background Color (the two blues you selected in the previous project) are used instead of black and white.

4 Using either the slider in the Navigator palette or the Zoom tool (🔍), zoom out so that the image covers less than a quarter of the width of the image window.

5 Select the Move tool (▶⊕), and drag the side handles for Layer 1 to stretch it so that it is about three times as wide as the image. Then click Commit (✔) in the tool options bar to accept the change.

You can zoom in again so that the image fills the window. (Try double-clicking the Hand tool to do this, or use another method.)

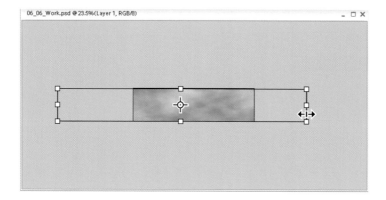

2 Drag the Background layer to New Layer (⬒) in the Layers palette to create another new layer, Background Copy. (Or, choose Layer > Duplicate Layer and accept the default layer name.)

3 Choose File > Save As, and then save the file in Photoshop (PSD) format as **06_07_Work**. Select the My CIB Work folder in the Lessons folder as the location. If Save In Version Set With Original is selected, be sure to deselect it before you click Save.

Now you're ready to start working.

Using the Healing Brush tool

You'll going to do something unusual and slightly disconcerting in this procedure, as you'll discover as you go through the steps. Be brave, and do not panic! The end result will be smoother skin and natural-looking skin tones.

1 Select the Healing Brush tool ( ), which is grouped with the Spot Healing Brush tool ( ) in the toolbox.

2 In the tool options bar, select the following options:

• For Brush, click the small arrow to open the pop-up palette and set the Diameter at approximately 15-20 px.

• For Mode, select Normal.

- For Source, select Sampled.

- Deselect Aligned and Use All Layers if they are selected.

3 Alt-click the Healing Brush tool in the center of the blurry green area on the left side of the image to establish that area as the reference texture.

Note: Until you perform this essential step, the Healing Brush tool can't work. If you switch to another tool and then back to the Healing Brush, you must repeat this step.

4 Drag a short distance around the wrinkles under the woman's eyes. As you drag, it looks as if you're painting green bags under the woman's eyes. When you release the mouse button, the green disappears and skin tones fill in the area.

Note: Be very careful to keep your brush strokes short. Longer strokes may produce unacceptable results. If that happens, choose Edit > Undo Healing Brush or use the Undo History palette to backtrack. Or, try just clicking instead of dragging. Also, make sure that Aligned is not selected in the tool options bar.

5 Continue to use the Healing Brush to smooth out the deep wrinkles and fine lines on the woman's forehead, face, hands, and neck. Avoid the areas close to the eyes or near the edges of her face.

Use the Undo History palette to quickly undo a series of steps. Every action you perform on the file is recorded in chronological order from top to bottom of the palette. To restore the file to an earlier state, simply select that action in the Undo History palette. If you change your mind before making any other changes, you can select a later step in the Undo History palette and restore the image to that phase of your work.

Admit it—you were surprised when your first stroke with the healing brush didn't paint a wide swath of green around the woman's eye. Most users share your reaction at first. If there had been an area of smooth skin, that would have been a good place to use as the source, but there wasn't.

The Healing Brush tool copies texture, not color. In this case, it samples the *colors* from only the area it brushes (the wrinkled skin) but arranges those colors according to the *texture* of the reference area (the blurry green). Consequently, the Healing Brush appears to be ironing the wrinkles right off the woman's crinkled skin. So far, the results are not convincingly realistic, but you'll work on that in the next topic.

Refining the healing work

There are numerous ways to smooth out textures in Photoshop Elements 3.0. Only a few of these powerful techniques are presented in this book.

In this topic, you'll employ another texture tool to finish your work on this image.

1 When you have wiped out the largest wrinkles, use the Navigator palette to zoom in and shift the focus to the eye area of the woman's face.

2 Select the Blur tool ( ). Then set the brush diameter in the tool options bar to approximately **13 px**.

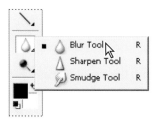

3 Drag the Blur tool over the fine wrinkles around the woman's eyes and mouth.

4 In the tool options bar, reduce the Blur tool brush diameter to about 7 or 8 px. Drag across the woman's lips to smooth them out, avoiding the edges.

5 Using the Healing Brush and Blur tools, continue working on the image until you have eradicated most of the wrinkles, fine lines, and age spots from the woman's face and hands. Use the Navigator palette to change the zoom level and shift the focus as needed.

6 In the Layers palette, change the Opacity of the Background Copy layer to about 70%, using your own judgment to set the exact percentage.

Compare your results to the original, retouched (100% Opacity), and final results illustrated below.

7 Choose File > Save, and then close the file.

Extensive retouching can leave skin looking artificially smooth, like molded plastic. Reducing the opacity of the retouched layer gives the woman's skin a more realistic look by allowing some of the wrinkles (on the original Background layer) to show through. Although they are slightly visible, the flaws are softened.

Congratulations! You've successfully completed another project. In this project, you learned how to set an appropriate source for the Healing Brush tool, and then use the texture of that source to repair flaws in another area of the photograph. You also used the Blur tool to smooth textures and finished with an opacity change, to create a more realistic look.

Project 8: Restoring a damaged photograph

All sorts of nasty things can happen to precious old photographs—or precious new photographs, to be fair about it. The scanned image you'll use in this project is challenging, to put it mildly, because of a large crease in the original print and other flaws. But if you think this is a hopeless case, that's where you'd be wrong.

With Photoshop Element 3.0 tools and features, you have the power to restore this picture to a convincing simulation of its original condition. Granted, there's no magic pill that fixes this kind of damage in one or two keystrokes, but it's not beyond your skill level. For important heirloom pictures, it's worth the effort, and we think you'll be impressed with what you can accomplish in this project.

Preparing a working copy of the image file

Your first job is to set up the file and layers for the work you'll do in this project.

1 Use the File Browser or Organizer to find and open the 06_08 file in Standard Edit.

2 Choose File > Save As.

3 In the Save As dialog box, type **06_08_Work** as the File Name and select Photoshop (PSD) as the Format. For Save In, select the My CIB Work folder in the Lessons folder. If Save In Version Set With Original is selected, be sure to deselect it before you click Save.

4 Choose Layer > Duplicate Layer and accept the default name (or drag the Background layer to the New Layer icon (◨) in the Layers palette) to create a Background Copy layer.

5 Choose File > Save.

You're ready to start repairing the image.

Using the Selection Brush tool

The first thing you'll do with this project is to use the Dust & Scratches filter to remove the stray dots and frayed edges of the scanned image. This filter smooths out the pixels in a way that puts the image just slightly out of focus. That's OK for the background, but you want to keep the subject matter—the children—as detailed and sharp as possible.

To do that, you'll need to create a selection that includes only the areas that it's OK to blur.

1 In the toolbox, select the Selection Brush tool (✐), being careful not to select one of the painting brush tools by mistake.

2 In the tool options bar, select a round brush shape and about 60 pixels for Size.

Leave the other options at the default values: Selection for Mode and 100% for Hardness.

3 Drag the brush along the frayed edges of the photograph to select those areas. Then increase the brush size to approximately 100 pixels, and continue painting the selection to include all the frayed edges and most of the backdrop behind the children.

Note: Don't try to be too precise; it's even OK if some of your strokes slop over onto the children because you'll fix that in the next topic.

4 Choose Select > Save Selection.

5 Name the new selection **Backdrop**, and click OK to close the dialog box.

The Selection Brush tool is an intuitive way to create a complex selection. It is especially useful in images like this one, where there are no unique color blocks, few sharp boundaries between pictured items, and few crisp geometric shapes.

What is a mask?

A mask is the opposite of a selection. The selection is the area that you can alter; everything outside the selection is unaffected by editing changes. A mask is the area that's protected from changes, just like the solid areas of a stencil or the masking tape you'd put on window glass before you paint the trim on your home.

Another difference between a mask and a selection is the way Photoshop Elements presents them visually. You're familiar with the flashing line of black and white dashes that signal a selection marquee. A mask appears as a colored, semi-transparent overlay on the image. You can change the color of the mask overlay using the Overlay Color option that appears in the tool options bar when the Selection Brush tool is set to operate in Mask mode.

Another advantage of the Selection Brush tool is that it is very forgiving. For example, you can hold down Alt to reverse the action, so that it removes areas from the selection rather than adding them to it. Or, you can use the tool in Mask mode, which is another intuitive way of adding to the areas outside the selection, as you'll try next.

Refining a saved selection

As you progress through this book, you are gathering lots of experience with saving selections. In this procedure, you'll amend a saved selection. You could then save the edited selection as a new selection, but instead you'll replace the original, saved selection with your improved version of it.

1 In the work area, make sure that:

• The Backdrop selection is still active in the image window. (If it is not active, choose Selection > Load Selection, and choose the saved selection by name before clicking OK.)

• The Selection Brush tool ( ) is still selected in the toolbox.

2 In the tool options bar, select Mask in the Mode pop-up menu.

You now see a semi-transparent, colored overlay in the *unselected* areas of the image. This represents the image *mask*, which covers the protected areas.

3 Examine the image, looking for unmasked areas with details that should be protected, such as places where the Selection Brush strokes lapped over onto the children.

If it helps to zoom in, use the Navigator palette slider or Zoom tool to adjust your view of the image.

4 Reduce the brush size of the Selection Brush to about 30 px, and paint to include any areas you want to mask.

In this mode, the Selection Brush tool adds to the mask rather than to the selection.

5 Switch back and forth between Selection and Mask modes, making corrections until you are satisfied that the rough selection is good enough.

Note: Your goal is to mask areas that contain fine details, even those caught in the crease. Although these are damaged, you can take advantage of the details that have survived.

6 Choose Select > Save Selection.

7 In the Save Selection dialog box, choose Backdrop from the Selection pop-up menu. Then, under Operation, select Replace Selection, and click OK.

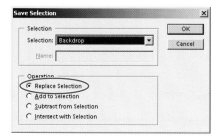

Filtering flaws out of the backdrop area

Now that you've made your selection, you're ready to apply the filter that will soften the selected areas, reducing the tiny scratches and dust specs.

1 If the Backdrop selection is no longer active, choose Select > Load Selection, and choose Backdrop before you click OK to close the dialog box.

2 Choose Filter > Noise > Dust & Scratches.

3 In the dialog box, make sure that Preview is selected, and then drag the Radius slider to 7 pixels and the Threshold slider to 10 levels. Move the dialog box so that you can see most of the image window, but do not close the dialog box yet.

4 Examine the results in the image window. The frayed edges of the image should be repaired and the stray dust and tiny scratches eliminated. (Move the pointer inside the thumbnail and drag with the hand icon to change the view area.)

5 Make adjustments to the Radius and Threshold values until you are satisfied with the results, and then click OK.

6 Choose Select > Deselect, and then save your work (File > Save).

The Dust & Scratches filter does a good job of clearing away spots created by flaws on the negative. However, it doesn't repair damage to the areas outside the selection.

Using the Clone Stamp tool to fill in missing areas

The Clone Stamp tool works in ways similar to the Healing Brush tool that you used in the previous project, when you removed wrinkles from a woman's face. The Clone Stamp tool copies the source area—not just texture—and places it in the areas where you drag.

In this procedure, you'll use the Clone Stamp tool to fill in missing details in the image from other, similar parts of the picture.

1 Using the Navigator palette slider or the Zoom tool, zoom in and focus on the bottom of the photograph in the area showing the boy's legs and feet, which is damaged by a heavy crease.

2 In the toolbox, select the Clone Stamp tool (🔖), which is grouped with the Pattern Stamp tool. Then click the tool icon (🔖) on the left end of the tool options bar to open a pop-up menu, and choose Reset Tool.

Reset Tool reinstates the default values: 21 px for Size, Normal for Mode, 100% for Opacity, and only Aligned selected.

3 Move the Clone Stamp tool so that it is centered at the edge of the shaded area between the boy's shoes. Hold down Alt and click to set the source position.

Centering the source on a horizontal stripe makes it easier to line up the brush for cloning.

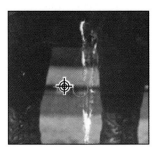

4 Move the brush over the damaged area so that it is centered at the same horizontal position as the source reference point. Then drag a short distance to copy the source image onto the damaged area.

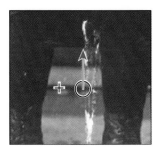

As you drag, crosshairs appear, indicating where the *source* is—that is, the area that the Clone Stamp tool is copying.

5 Drag the brush vertically over the crease-damaged area until the repair is complete.

The crosshairs follow the movement of the brush. Because you selected the Aligned option in the tool options bar, the crosshairs maintain the same distance and angle to the brush as you set when you made the first brush stroke.

Note: *If necessary, you can reset the source by Alt-clicking again.*

6 Choose File > Save.

Cleaning the girl's shoes

Through no fault of the photographer, the white shoes on the little girl appear scuffed and dirty. You'll tidy them up with the Dodge tool.

The Dodge tool and its opposite, the Burn tool, derive their names from traditional darkroom techniques for controlling the exposure for different areas of an image. In this task, you'll use the electronic equivalent of *dodging* (reducing the exposure for a limited area of the light-sensitive photographic paper).

1 Using the Navigator palette or scroll bars, shift the focus to the little girl's feet. Keep the zoom level high enough that you can see details easily, such as the texture of her stockings.

2 In the toolbox, select the Dodge tool ( ).

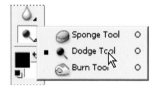

3 In the tool options bar, select a soft round brush and set the Size to a small diameter, such as 19 or 20 pixels. Make sure that Midtones and 50% Exposure are selected.

4 Drag the Dodge tool across one of the dirty toes on the girl's shoes, using short brush strokes.

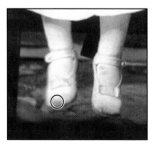

5 Continue to apply the Dodge tool until the toes of the shoes look about the same as the clean parts.

Finishing up the project

Only your available time and patience limit how much clean-up work you do on old photographs. You could spend longer working on this picture, but the quality now is acceptable for most purposes. You'll fix just a few more areas before leaving this project.

1 Double-click the Hand tool ( ) to zoom out so that you can see the entire image. (Or, use the Navigator palette or the Zoom tool.)

2 Examine the entire image, looking for dark or light flecks created by dust on the negative, especially on the boy's jacket.

3 In the toolbox, select the Blur tool ( ), and type **40** px for Size in the tool options bar.

4 Click or drag the tool over any dust spots to blend them into the area surrounding them.

5 Review all areas of the image. If you see flaws that you want to fix, use the Blur tool, Dodge tool, or Clone Stamp tool to make those repairs or corrections until you tire of it.

6 Choose File > Save, and then close the file.

Good work! In this project, you've used blurring and a filter to hide spots, flecks, and texture flaws. You've also cloned one area of an image to fill in a similar area that's been lost or damaged. You've used the Selection Brush tool to create selections in two modes: Selection and Mask. Along the way, you've seen how to reset a tool to its default settings.

Saving and organizing your finished files

If you've finished earlier lessons in this book, you're familiar with this final phase of the lesson: adding tags to the work files.

1 Click Photo Browser ( ) on the Photoshop Elements Editor shortcuts bar to switch to Organizer. If Back To All Photos appears above the thumbnails, select it.

2 Choose Find > Untagged Items.

3 Choose Edit > Select All, or press Ctrl + A to select all the thumbnails.

4 Drag the Work Files tag and then the Lesson 6 tag to the thumbnails to apply them.

5 (Optional) Use Edit > Stack > Stack Selected Photos to stack the Weather project 1 and Weather project 2 work files. Repeat for Weather projects 5 and 6.

You can now select Back To All Photos to see the entire catalog of thumbnails.

Congratulations again! You've now finished with Lesson 6.

Review questions

1 Describe two ways to copy a layer from one image file into another.

2 Can you delete areas of the Background or change its position in the layer stack? Can you make another layer the Background?

3 What is the purpose of the Eyedropper tool?

4 What action is necessary before you can start using either the Clone Stamp tool or the Healing Brush tool?

Review answers

1 One method is to select the Move tool and drag from one image window to the other. The other method is to drag the layer from the Layers palette for the first image into the image window for the second image. If you use this technique, it is not necessary to select the Move tool. No matter which method you use, you must be able to see at least part of both images in the work area, so Maximize Mode cannot be active (on the Window > Images submenu). Also, if you hold down Shift as you drag, the new layer will be centered in the image.

2 No to both questions. The changes you can make to the special Background layer are limited. However, changing the name of the Background layer (by double-clicking it in the Layers palette and clicking OK in the message that appears) converts the Background into an ordinary layer. You can then delete areas, transform, move up or down the layer stack, and apply other layer changes. Although another layer can replace the former Background layer at the bottom of the layer stack, that does not impose limitations on it. Even renaming a layer *Background* does not reinstate the special protections associated with the original Background.

3 The Eyedropper tool is a great way to select a color that's in an image and set that color as the Foreground or Background color. You click the image at the spot where the color you want appears, and the Eyedropper tool picks it up.

4 Both tools copy from one part of an image to another. Before you can start copying, you have to define the source of the copying. You do that by holding down Alt and then clicking the area of the image that you want to use as the source. Then you can drag the tool over the area where you want to reproduce the texture (Healing Brush) or image (Clone Stamp).

7 Adding Emphasis

This lesson gives you a taste of the many ways of drawing the viewer's eye to an area. Whether you want to set off your image in a frame, emphasize an area of the photograph, or underscore an idea, you'll find the right tools in Photoshop Elements 3.0.

In this lesson, you will learn how to do the following:

- Frame images in various ways, from easy to moderately complex.

- Make highly refined selections.

- Clear unwanted background colors from areas of an image.

- Scale a layer.

- Colorize an area, creating a monochromatic color scheme.

- Create and save a custom pattern.

- Distort a layer to create a perspective.

This lesson consists of seven, independent projects, each involving a different image file. Allow about two hours total for the entire lesson, or break it up into shorter work sessions.

Although you can do this lesson out of order, Lesson 7 requires some file structures, custom tags, and skills covered in Lessons 1 and 2 and the project files from the CD attached to the back of this book. See "Copying the Classroom in a Book files" on page 3.

Getting started

The first five projects in this lesson demonstrate different ways to add a frame to an image. Each of these procedures is relatively easy and short. The final two projects show how to add emphasis to an area of the image, either by toning down everything in the picture except the area you want to emphasize or by repetition.

1 Start Photoshop Elements 3.0 in Standard Edit mode.

2 Open the Palette and Photo Bins, if they are not already open, by clicking the arrows (▮▶) and (▲) at the bottom of the work area or by choosing Window > Palette Bin and Window > Photo Bin to place check marks on those commands.

3 Review the contents of the Palette Bin, making sure that the Layers, Navigator, Styles And Effects, and Undo History palettes are there.

Note: For help with Palette Bin contents, see "Using the Palette Bin" on page 59.

4 Click Photo Browser (⊞) on the shortcuts bar to switch to Organizer.

You can start with almost any project in this lesson, because they are independent of each other in both subject matter and skill level. However, Projects 4, 6, and 7 are more time-consuming than the others.

Framing images

A good way to draw attention to an image is to frame it. With Photoshop Elements, you can draw great-looking frames around images with very little effort, thanks to the many built-in features and effects available to you. Use the results for your web pages, electronic scrapbooks, or e-cards. Or, import them into an advertisement or newsletter created in a page-layout application, such as Adobe InDesign®, Adobe PageMaker®, or Adobe FrameMaker®.

The first projects in this lesson explore just a few of the frame effects you can create. In every case, you should learn something new about techniques and potential uses for Photoshop Elements.

Note: The five framing projects in this lesson use specific images. However, in most cases you can substitute some of your own photographs as you do these first five exercises.

Project 1: Printing images in a temporary frame

One of the simplest ways to add frames takes place when you're ready to print. Unlike the other frames you'll create in this section, this type of frame does not become a permanent part of the image file. Consequently, you can work with the original image files rather than creating work copies, because the files themselves will not change.

Before you begin, make sure that Photoshop Elements is open in Organizer. (See "Getting started" on page 228.)

1 On the Tags tab in the Organize Bin, expand the Lessons category, and select the Find box for the Lesson 7 tag. Then expand the Projects category and select the Find box for the Project 1 tag.

2 Choose Edit > Select All (or press Ctrl + A) to select the three thumbnails.

3 Choose File > Print.

4 Choose the following for the pop-up menus on the right side of the Print Selected Photos dialog box (some of which are numbered):

• For (1) Select Printer, choose any available printer, or leave your default printer selected.

• For (2) Select Type Of Print, choose Picture Package. If a message appears warning you about print resolution, click OK.

- For (3) Select A Layout, choose Letter (4) 4x5.

- For Select A Frame, choose Classic Oval.

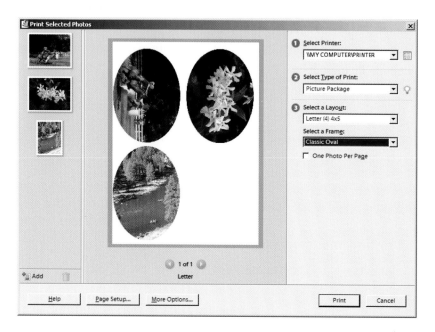

Leave the dialog box open for the next steps.

Note: *Instead of Classic Oval, you can try other choices on the Select A Frame menu, such as Green Plaid or Color Swirl. (You have dozens of frame styles to explore.)*

5 In the lower left area of the dialog box, click Add.

6 In the Add Photos dialog box, select the Entire Catalog option, and then select the check box for one of the images to select it. (You don't have to use the same image shown in the example.) Then click OK. If another warning message appears, click OK.

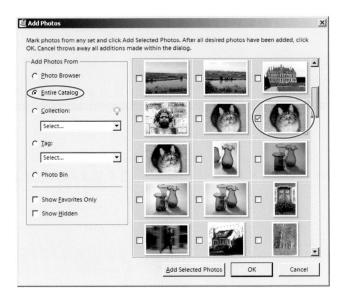

7 Do one of the following:

• Click Print if you want to print the images. *(Not recommended.)*

• Click Cancel to return to Organizer without printing the images.

Note: The sample images are low-resolution, so the print would probably be of low quality. It's a better idea to use your own photographs for any actual printing.

The framing options in the Print dialog box are handy for quick jobs where it's OK if all the frames are the same. In other cases, you may want to use more elegant frames or to frame individual images differently from others on the same print-out page. Either of these requires more complex procedures, such as the ones you'll try in the next four projects.

Do you want to print multiple copies of a photo on a single page—like the school portraits that you had to cut apart yourself? Select Picture Package in the Print Selected Photos dialog box, choose a layout with the sizes and numbers of prints you want to make, and then select One Photo Per Page. (One Photo Per Page fills the layout with multiple prints of one picture rather than one print each of multiple picture.)

Project 2: Adding a simple frame to an image

Photoshop Elements 3.0 features a variety of Effects that you can apply to an image, including several types of frames. In this project, you'll surround the image with a colored frame, using the current Foreground Color. Unlike the previous project, this type of frame becomes a permanent part of the saved image file.

1 In Photoshop Elements Organizer, use the Lesson 7 and Project 2 tags to find the image for this project (a flowerbox outside a window).

2 Select the thumbnail, click Edit (▩), and choose Go To Standard Edit.

3 Do one of the following to select a Foreground Color for the frame:

• Choose Window > Color Swatches, and select a color swatch in that palette.

• Click the Foreground Color swatch in the toolbox to open the Color Picker, and select a color.

• Select the Eyedropper tool (🖋) in the toolbox, and click a color within the photograph itself to pick up that color. (The example used this method to pick up the color of the wood sashing around the window panes, but you can choose any color you want.)

4 In the Styles And Effects palette, do the following:

• Choose Effects and Frames in the pop-up menus at the top of the palette.

• Double-click the Foreground Color Frame thumbnail to apply it to the image. Or, you can drag the thumbnail onto the image window.

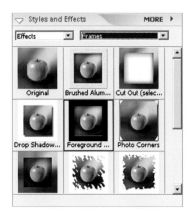 

5 Do one of the following:

• If you are not satisfied with the results, choose Edit > Undo Foreground Color Frame, and go back to Step 3.

• If the frame is acceptable to you, choose File > Save As.

6 In the Save As dialog box, select the My CIB Work folder in the Lessons folder, type **07_02_Work** as the file name, and choose Photoshop (PSD) as the Format. Then click Save.

You can close the file when you are ready to go on to the next project.

The Foreground Color Frame effect automatically adds a frame to the image, increasing the dimensions of the canvas. The frame already has a subtle bevel and a drop shadow that give it a realistic appearance.

Project 3: Creating a vignette effect in an image file

Another difference between the frames you add in the Picture Package Print dialog box and frame Effects you apply in Standard Edit mode is complexity. In the Print dialog box, you can select only one frame style. In Editor, you can apply multiple Effects to an image. In this project, you'll apply a vignette. Although the instructions stop there, you could use the resulting file as the basis for other frame effects available in Photoshop Elements 3.0.

1 Use the File Browser or Organizer to find and open the 07_03 file (a swan in a pond) in Standard Edit mode.

2 In the toolbox, select the Elliptical Marquee tool (○), which is grouped with the Rectangular Marquee tool (▢). In the tool options bar, type **10 px** for Feather.

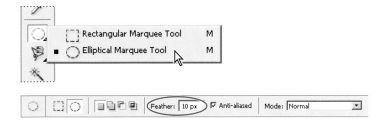

3 Drag a selection oval that is large enough to enclose the swan.

Note: *If the selection is not centered, move the pointer inside the selection so that its appearance changes (**), and drag the selection marquee into place. If the selection shape or size isn't what you want, redo the selection.*

4 In the Styles And Effects palette for Effects and Frames, double-click the Vignette (Selection) thumbnail, or drag the thumbnail to the image window.

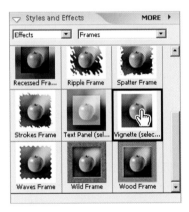

5 Examine the results, and do one of the following:

• Choose Edit > Undo Vignette (Selection), and go back to Step 4.

• Choose File > Save As, and save the file as **07_03_Work** in Photoshop (PSD) format, saving it in the My CIB Work folder in the Lessons folder. Then close the file.

That's it—you're done with this project.

Feathering softens the edge of a selection. You can set the Feather value to zero pixels when you want a hard, sharp edge, or you can use a larger number to have the selection edge change gradually.

Project 4: Drawing a frame with the Custom Shape tool

You've already used the Custom Shape tool when you created a cartoon-like talk balloon in Lesson 2. In this project, you'll use a different custom shape and then use a related tool, the Cookie Cutter. The difference between the two boils down to what goes inside the shape. The Custom Shape tool fills the shape with the Foreground Color. The Cookie Cutter tool fills the shape with existing pixels on the selected layer, cutting away the rest of that layer.

The image for this exercise is a photograph that has already been posterized (using Filter > Adjustments > Posterize). This process reduces the number of component colors and gives the image an interesting look.

1 Using the File Browser or Organizer, find, select, and open the 07_04 file (the spout of a fountain, shaped like a face) in Standard Edit.

2 Use the Eyedropper tool (✐) to select a color for the frame from any part of the image.

3 Select the Custom Shape tool (◯). In the tool options bar, click the small arrow by Shapes to open the Shapes Picker. Then click the arrow (◉) to open the palette menu, and choose Frames. Finally, double-click the Frame 15 thumbnail in the Shapes Picker.

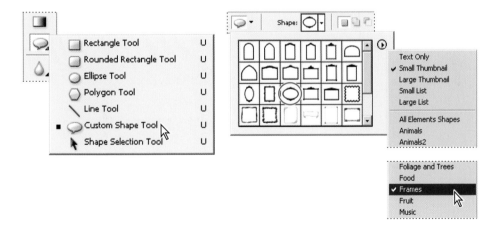

4 Drag a frame around the face, starting in the upper left quadrant of the image. Leave Shape 1 selected for the next step.

Note: If you want to color the shape differently, use the Color option in the tool options bar to select another color. If it is the wrong size or not positioned correctly, select the Move tool (⯒₊), and drag the frame or its boundary corners to move or resize it.

5 In the Styles And Effects palette, choose Layer Styles and Bevels in the two pop-up menus, and then double-click the Inner Ridge thumbnail to apply it to the shape.

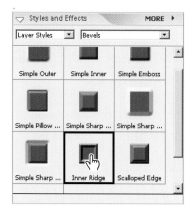

6 In the Layers palette, select the Background layer.

7 In the toolbox, select the Cookie Cutter tool (🍪), and do the following:

• Type **0 px** as the Feather amount, if it is not already selected.

• Open the Shapes Picker, click the arrow (◉) to open the palette menu, and choose Shapes. Then scroll down the Shapes Picker as needed, and select the thumbnail for the solid black circle.

• Drag diagonally to draw a circle that fits in between the ridges of the frame shape. Use the handles on the bounding box to adjust the size and placement of the circle. Then click Commit (✔).

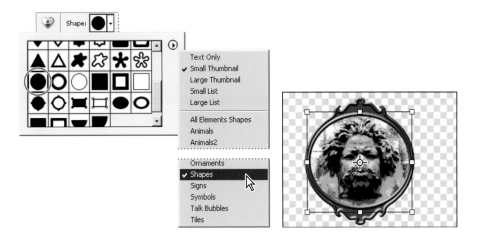

8 Choose File > Save For Web. Select GIF 32 No Dither from the Preset pop-up menu, and select Transparency. Then click OK.

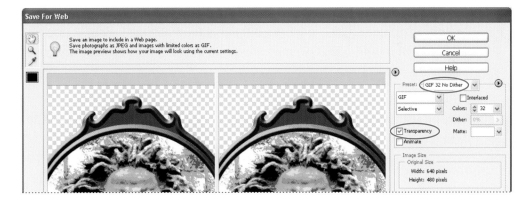

9 In the Save Optimized As dialog box, save the file as **Fountain.gif** in the My CIB Work folder in your Lessons folder.

10 Choose File > Save, and save the file in Photoshop PSD format in the My CIB Work.

Your choice of GIF 32 reduces the number of colors used in the image to 32. Because the original image was posterized, the number of colors was already limited, so there was no lessening of image quality. GIF also preserves the transparency in the image.

Project 5: Framing the image with itself

So far, you've used automatic features to frame images. In this procedure, you'll create a frame manually, but the process is almost as easy as creating an automatic frame. The following procedure uses layers to create a frame-like look that can be effective for greeting cards, posters, and other uses.

1 Using the File Browser or Organizer, find and open the 07_05 file (a village steeple) in Standard Edit.

2 Create a copy of the Background layer by dragging the layer to the New Layer icon (◩) or by choosing Layer > Duplicate Layer.

3 Choose Image > Resize > Scale.

Note: If the Scale command is not available, make sure that the Background Copy layer is selected in the Layers palette, or select it now and try again.

4 In the tool options bar, type **80%** in W, and select Maintain Aspect Ratio (◉) to automatically enter 80% as the H value.

💡 *Instead of typing, you can scrub to set the width percentage: Position the pointer over the W so that it turns into a pointing hand with arrows (👆), and drag horizontally to change the value.*

5 Select the Background layer, and choose Enhance > Adjust Lighting > Brightness/Contrast. Move the Brightness slider to +30 before you click OK.

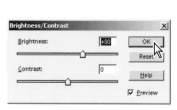

6 Choose File > Save As, and save the file as **07_05_Work** in Photoshop (PSD) format, saving it in the My CIB Work folder in the Lessons folder.

7 Choose File > Close.

The Scale command resizes only the selected layer, not the entire image. Other commands on the Resize submenu apply to the whole image file.

Congratulations! You've now finished the last of the five framing projects. If you've done them all, you've produced five different types of frames. In the course of completing these exercises, you've gained expertise in the use of Effects, Filters, and Layer Styles, all of which appear in the Styles And Effects palette. You've also resized a layer without changing the overall dimensions of the image itself and had more opportunities to work with the Eyedropper tool.

Project 6: Stylizing to focus attention

Your next project is pure fun. That is, it has nothing to do with creating a more realistic picture and everything to do with beguiling your audience. You'll work on a photograph of a large bear peering around the trunk of an evergreen tree. In this image, the colors are uniformly intense and interesting, so the picture lacks a clear focus.

You'll add drama to the scene by muting everything except the animal. You'll do this by neutralizing the colors and blurring the surrounding area in a way that draws even more attention to the bear.

Selecting a complex shape

It's rarely possible to select a complex shape in a single action. Usually, you'll need to make refinements after your initial selection. If you've completed earlier lessons in this book, you've already gained experience in doing this, such as when you created the selections of the truck (in Lesson 3), of the leafy sky area next to the pillar (in Lesson 4), and of the two children (in Lesson 6).

For most selection tools, you can add to or subtract from a selection (rather than start a new one), either by holding down a keyboard key as you select or by activating the appropriate selection type in the tool options bar.

Important*: Before you begin this topic, make sure that you have enough time to complete it and the next one before you take a break—about 15 minutes. If you don't complete the selection process and save the selection before you end your work session, you could lose all the hard work you've done.*

1 In the File Browser or Organizer, find, select, and open the 07_06.jpg file (a bear standing by a tree) in Standard Edit mode.

2 Select the Lasso tool (⌇) in the toolbox, and drag the lasso around the bear, maintaining a small distance between the bear and its background so that some of the snow and tree are also selected.

Note: *The Polygonal Lasso tool may be shown in the toolbox. If so, hold down the mouse button on the tool icon and select the Lasso tool from the list, or select it and then select the Lasso tool icon in the tool options bar.*

💡 *You can release the Lasso tool before you get back to the starting point of the selection you're drawing. The tool will complete the shape by adding a straight line between the starting point and the point at which you released the mouse button.*

3 Select the Magic Wand tool (⭐). In the tool options bar, type **32** for Tolerance, and make sure that Contiguous is selected.

4 If necessary, hold down Alt to change the tool pointer so that it includes a tiny minus sign (✸), and click inside the existing selection on one of the blue or white areas of snow behind the bear. Repeat for other blue or white areas of the selection—always being careful to keep the Alt key pressed—until you have removed all of the snow from the selection.

Note: Don't try to select the small white patch between the tree and the bear's ear. It may be easier to deal with this area using the Lasso tool when you do Steps 5-7.

5 Use the Zoom tool, Navigator palette slider, or View menu commands to increase the zoom level to about 150%.

6 Select the Lasso tool (᳇), and then select the Subtract From Selection icon (᳇) in the tool options bar (so that you don't have to hold down Alt to subtract).

7 Drag the pointer around a small area of tree within this existing selection, trying precisely to follow the border between the bear and the tree or the snow.

Note: If Step 6 does not remove the area from the selection as expected, choose Edit > Undo Lasso, or press Ctrl + Z. Then make sure you have the Subtract From Selection icon selected in the tool options bar, as described in Step 5. Also, make sure that the Snap To Grid command is not selected on the View menu. Then try again to remove part of the selection.

8 Continue to remove the tree trunk from the selection, one small area after another, until only the bear remains in the selection, using the Lasso tool.

You may need to zoom in even farther to make a reasonably accurate selection around the claws of the animal, or you may want to switch to the Add To Selection option in the tool options bar (⬚), if you remove an area that should be part of the selection.

Go directly to the next procedure so that you don't accidentally lose your selection.

Saving the bear selection

You've gone to considerable trouble to create the bear selection, so it's a good idea to save it now. Then, if you are interrupted or distracted and lose the selection, you can reload the saved selection and resume your work.

1 With the selection from the previous procedure still active, choose Select > Save Selection.

2 In the dialog box, name the new selection **Bear**, and click OK.

3 Choose File > Save.

4 In the Save As dialog box, navigate to the My CIB Work folder. Type **07_06_Work** for File Name, and click Save.

This couldn't be simpler, but having the saved selection can save you loads of time if you need to backtrack.

Blurring the background

Now that your painstakingly made selection is safely stored, it's time to put it to good use.

The previous procedures asked you to select the bear rather than the background area and the tree, which are the parts of the picture that you want to alter. The reason for this approach is that the bear is easier to select. Once you've done that, you can simply turn the selection inside out to protect the bear while you apply changes to the rest of the picture.

1 Invert the Bear selection by doing one of the following:

• If the selection is still active, choose Select > Inverse.

• If the selection is no longer active, choose Select > Load Selection, choose Bear, select the Invert check box, and click OK.

Because you selected the Invert option or Inverse command, everything *except* the bear is selected in the image window: the tree, the snow, and the rocks.

2 Choose Filter > Blur > Radial Blur.

3 In the Radial Blur dialog box, do the following:

• Drag the Amount slider to 30.

• Select Zoom as the Blur Method.

• In the Blur Center thumbnail, drag the center slightly up and to the left, so that it is in approximately the same position as the bear's head in the actual image.

- Review the selected options, and click OK.

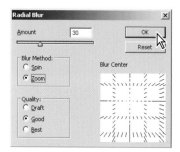

If possible, do not deselect. You'll use the selection again in the next topic. If you have to take a break, that's OK because you've saved the selection and can reload it when you resume work on the project.

By blurring the background, you de-emphasize that part of the picture. This shifts the focus to where you want it: on the bear. By selecting a radial blur, you also add drama to the scene. The rays created by the blurring act like arrows, drawing the eye to the center where the bear is.

Colorizing the background

You can draw even more attention to the bear by reducing the background colors to a monochromatic color scheme.

1 If the background area for the bear picture is not still selected, load and invert the Bear selection (Select > Load Selection, and select Invert and Bear).

2 Choose Enhance > Adjust Color > Adjust Hue/Saturation.

3 In the Hue/Saturation dialog box, do all of the following:

- Select the Colorize check box first.

- Drag the Hue slider or type **270**.

- Drag the Saturation slider or type **30**.

- Drag the Lightness slider or type **+30**.

- Select the Preview check box, if necessary, and take a look at the results in the image window. (Move the dialog box aside, if necessary.)

• Adjust the Hue, Saturation, and Lightness settings as needed until you are happy with the results, and then click OK.

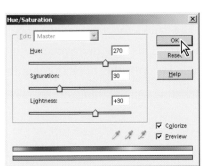

💡 *Pressing Ctrl + H hides the flashing marquee around the selection, so you can see the transition between the selected and unselected areas. If you use this, always be careful to press Ctrl + H again so that you can see the selection marquee and won't forget that a selection is active.*

4 Choose File > Save As, and save the file in the My CIB Work folder with its current name (07_06_Work) in Photoshop (PSD) format.

5 Close the file (File > Close).

Another triumph! You've completed this project and have a good-looking picture to prove it. In this procedure, you've gained experience in methods of making complex selections by using various selection tools to refine a rough selection. You've also used one of the blur filters to add drama to the scene, and colorized one area to emphasize a different area.

💡 *A similar way to create emphasis in a color picture is to desaturate an area (remove the color so that it looks like a black-and-white photograph). This makes the remaining colored objects pop out, immediately grabbing the viewer's attention. You can do this by selecting the area and setting the Saturation value to -100% in the Hue/Saturation dialog box instead of selecting Colorize and changing the Hue and Lightness values.*

Project 7: Emphasizing by repetition

If one picture of something you like is good, shouldn't more be even better? In this project, you'll use a photograph of a family pet to create a pattern. Then you'll use the pattern to create the impression of wallpaper within the original picture.

As you do this exercise, you can pick up some new tricks for changing the appearance of a layer by altering its position and perspective. You'll also get more practice in making selections and working with layers—two of the core skills this book is committed to helping you master.

Making a selection to use as a pattern

In this procedure, you'll use three different techniques for making a selection. All three methods are familiar to you from various earlier projects in this book.

1 In the File Browser or Organizer, find and open the 07_07 file (a resting dog) in Standard Edit.

2 Select the Elliptical Marquee tool (◯) and type **0 px** for Feather in the tool options bar. Then drag a roughly circular shape that includes the puppy's face and ears.

3 Select the Magic Wand tool (✎), and select Subtract From Selection (▣) in the tool options bar. Make sure that Tolerance is 32 and Contiguous is selected.

4 Click the painted wall area that is inside the selection marquee to remove it from the selection. (One click should be all you need.)

5 Select the Zoom tool (🔍), and select Zoom In (🔍) in the tool options bar. Then drag a rectangle around the selection to zoom in so that the rectangular area fills the image window.

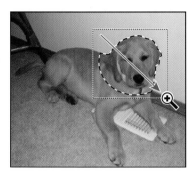

6 Select the Selection Brush tool (🖌). In the tool options bar, set **20 px** for Size, and choose Mask from the Mode pop-up menu.

7 Drag the Selection Brush as needed to extend the mask over everything except the dog's face and ears.

If necessary, hold down Alt and drag to erase areas of the mask that you want to remove. (Or, you can switch from Mask to Selection mode, and use the Selection Brush to extend the selection. But this selection doesn't need to be perfect for the purposes of this project.)

Now you're all set to define a custom pattern, so do not deselect before you go on to the next procedure. If you are interrupted now or have to take a break, you can save the selection and then load it later, as you've done before in several earlier projects.

Defining a custom pattern

You're going to create a pattern based on the selection you made in the previous procedure, "Making a selection to use as a pattern." If that area (the dog's face and ears) is no longer selected, go back and do that procedure again.

1 With the dog's face and ears still selected, choose Edit > Copy, or press Ctrl + C.

2 Choose Edit > Paste, or press Ctrl + V.

In the Layers palette, a new layer appears, Layer 1. The layer thumbnail shows that the layer is transparent except for the copy of the dog's head.

Note: *If the layer thumbnail is a generic brush ( ), click the More arrow at the top of the Layers palette, and choose Palette Options. Then select one of the three sizes for the layer thumbnail (but do not choose None).*

3 In the Layers palette, click the eye icon for the Background layer to hide it, and select Layer 1.

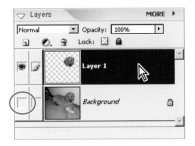

4 Choose Image > Resize > Scale. In the tool options bar, type **35%** in W and select Maintain Aspect Ratio ( ) to automatically enter 35% for H. Press Enter or click Commit (✔) to accept the new size of the dog's face.

5 Select the Rectangular Marquee tool ( ), which is grouped with the Elliptical Marquee tool you used in the previous procedure.

6 Hold down Shift (to constrain the selection to a square), and drag a square that encloses all of the dog's head fairly closely. If necessary, place the pointer inside the selection square and drag it into position.

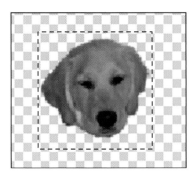

7 Choose Edit > Define Pattern From Selection. In the dialog box that appears, type **Stella**—that's the dog's name—as the pattern name, and click OK.

8 Choose Edit > Delete, or press the Delete key. Then deselect (Select > Deselect or press Ctrl + D).

If you were brave enough to do Step 8, you'll see that Layer 1 is completely empty. However, you will use this blank layer for another purpose in the next procedure.

Applying a custom pattern

You'll use the leftover blank layer from the previous project as the canvas on which you'll apply your custom pattern.

1 In the Navigator palette, drag the slider or click the Zoom Out icon on the left end of the slider until you can see the entire image area in the image window.

2 In the toolbox, select the Paint Bucket tool ( ).

3 In the tool options bar, select Pattern on the Fill pop-up menu.

4 If a thumbnail of the Stella pattern does not appear in the Pattern option, click the arrow to open the Pattern Picker, and select it now.

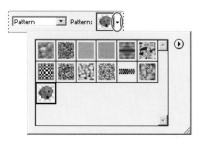

5 Make sure that Layer 1 is selected in the Layers palette, and then click the Paint Bucket anywhere in the image.

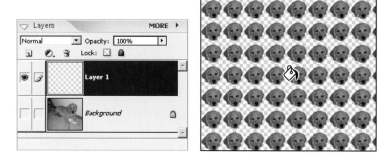

6 Click to place an eye icon (👁) in the Background layer so that it is visible, too.

💡 *The Paint Bucket tool isn't the only way to apply a pattern. You can also use the Pattern Stamp tool, which reveals the pattern bit by bit as you did with the Fishy Tales project in Lesson 2. The Paint Bucket is faster, and its coverage is complete.*

Distorting the pattern layer

The pattern currently sits squarely on top of the original image, which you can see through the transparent areas of the layer, between the dog faces. Your next objective is to align it with the wall in the image so that it looks more like wallpaper.

1 Using the Navigator palette slider, zoom out to about 35% so that you can see plenty of gray pasteboard around the image in the image window.

2 Select the Move tool (), and drag the layer so that the lower right corner is aligned with the top edge of the molding at the right edge of the picture.

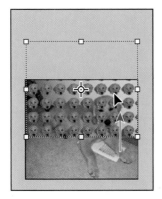

3 Choose Image > Transform > Distort.

4 Drag the corners of Layer 1 as follows:

• Drag the lower left corner up, to align it with the top of the molding on the left edge of the picture.

• Drag the upper right corner of the layer down, near the upper right corner of the image.

• Drag the upper left corner down a short distance—for just a hint of perspective.

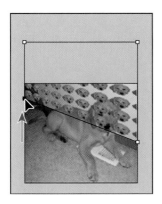 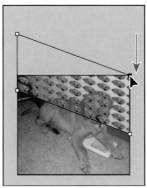 

5 When you are satisfied with the shape, click Commit (✔) or press Enter.

Placing the pattern behind the dog

The custom pattern layer is currently interfering with your view of the dog. Your next task is to make it look as if the pattern is behind the dog, like wallpaper on the wall.

1 In the Layers palette, select the Background layer, and choose Layer > Duplicate Layer. Click OK to accept the default name.

Or, drag the Background layer thumbnail to the New Layer icon (▣) in the Layers palette to create the duplicate layer.

2 Drag the new layer, Background Copy, to the top of the layer stack so that it blocks your view of the other two layers.

You can zoom in as needed, but be sure you can see the entire wall area.

3 Select the Magic Wand tool (✎) and make sure that Tolerance is 32 and Contiguous is selected in the tool options bar. Then click the grayish-white wall behind the dog to select an area of white paint.

4 In the tool options bar, select Add To Selection (⬚), so that when you move the pointer into the image, it includes a small plus (+) sign by the Magic Wand. Click the other areas of the wall until it is all selected, including the small area visible under the chair leg.

5 When you are satisfied with your selection of all the wall area, press Delete (or choose Edit > Delete) to erase the blank wall from the Background Copy layer.

6 Choose Select > Deselect (or press Ctrl + D).

7 Choose File > Save As, and name the file **07_07_Work**, saving it in Photoshop (PSD) format in the Lessons\My CIB Work folder.

This completes the work on the image itself. Before you finish your session, you'll do one more thing that could save you time and effort on projects of your own.

Saving a pattern in a custom pattern library

As long as you've gone to the trouble of creating a custom pattern, you might as well save it for future use. Who knows when it might come in handy?

1 In the toolbox, select the Paint Bucket tool ( ) so that the Patterns option is available in the tool options bar.

2 Open the Pattern Picker. Click the arrow button to open the palette menu, and choose Save Patterns.

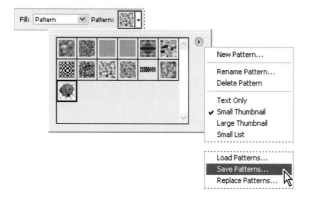

3 In the Save dialog box, type **My Custom Patterns** or another name of your choice. Leave the Location and Format as they are (in the Patterns folder for Photoshop Elements 3.0 and in Patterns (*.PAT) format.

4 Click Save.

5 Choose File > Close.

Your custom Stella pattern is now a permanent part of your Photoshop Elements application. Although the idea behind this project is rather silly and homespun, you could use a similar process to create serious business graphics. For example, you could create a pattern featuring your organization's logo or a product that your company sells. This kind of repetition can be an effective way of emphasizing identity for your web pages, stationery, or other documents.

You've successfully polished off another project. In this lesson, you've learned how to create and save custom patterns that you can quickly apply to images. You've also moved and distorted a layer, skewing it so that it looks as if it's plastered on the wall in the picture.

Congratulations, because you've not only finished the project, you've almost finished this lesson. All that remains is for you to organize your work files.

Saving and organizing your finished files

If you've already finished earlier lessons in this book, you are familiar with this final phase of the lesson. You're going to add tags to the work files, which were already added to the Organizer when you saved them, thanks to the Include In Organizer option in the Save As dialog box.

1 If necessary, click Photo Browser ( ) on the Photoshop Elements Editor shortcuts bar to switch to Organizer. If Back To All Photos appears above the thumbnails area, select it.

2 Choose Find > Untagged Items.

3 Choose Edit > Select All or press Ctrl + A to select all the thumbnails.

4 Drag the Work Files tag and then the Lesson 7 tag to the thumbnails to apply them.

5 Select the Back To All Photos button to see the entire catalog of thumbnails.

Good work! You've now completely finished Lesson 7. Turn to the review questions on the next page to test your mastery of the skills and techniques you've used.

Review questions

1 Do frames you select in the Print Photos dialog box become a permanent part of the image file? Are these frames available for all types of printing?

2 Name two sources of frame types that can be incorporated into the image file.

3 What is the difference between the Custom Shape tool and the Cookie Cutter tool? Between the Cookie Cutter tool and the Crop tool?

4 Describe the difference between changing the image size and scaling.

Review answers

1 No, the frames added in the Print Photos dialog box don't become part of the image file. So, you can print your favorite pictures with one frame for one occasion and a different frame for another. These frames are available only when Picture Package is selected for Select Type Of Print. They are not available for individual prints, contact sheets, or labels.

2 Frames selections are available in the Styles And Effects palette when Effects is selected in the first pop-up menu and either Frames or All is selected in the other pop-up menu. Frame selections are also available for the Custom Shape tool. You can find these selection by opening the Shape Picker from the tool options bar, and then clicking the arrow on the Shape Picker to open the palette menu, and choosing Frames.

3 Although the full set of Elements Shapes is available for both the Custom Shape tool and Cookie Cutter tool, the two tools produce different results. The Custom Shape tool draws the selected shape on a new layer, giving the shape the current Foreground Color. The Cookie Cutter tool deletes everything on the currently selected layer except the part of the image that's inside the shape. Other layers of the image are not affected. The Crop tool affects the entire image, changing the canvas size so that it includes only part of the original image. The Crop tool cuts only in rectangular shapes.

4 Scaling resizes only the layer that is currently selected in the Layers palette. The canvas size and the other layers remain unchanged. Changing the image size resizes all layers.

8 Combining Multiple Images

If you're ready to go beyond fixing individual pictures in conventional ways, this lesson is for you. In it, you'll venture into the world of multiple images to create amazing graphics from ordinary photographs.

In this lesson you will do the following:

- Copy and paste selected areas of one image into another.
- Resize the canvas area of an image.
- Define and use a specific width-height ratio for cropping.
- Scale a layer.
- Create a gradient from opaque to transparent.
- Apply a clipping path to an image layer.
- Paint on a layer.

This lesson includes four, independent projects, some of which you'll be able to complete in about 10 or 20 minutes; others may take as long as 45 minutes. In all, allow at least an hour and a half.

Getting started

Before you begin, make sure that your work area is set up according to the way the lessons are.

1 Start Photoshop Elements 3.0 Editor in Standard Edit mode.

2 Open the Palette and Photo Bins, if they are not already open, by clicking the arrows (◀▶) and (▲) at the bottom of the work area or by choosing Window > Palette Bin and Window > Photo Bin to place check marks on those commands.

3 Review the contents of the Palette Bin, making sure that the Layers, Navigator, Styles And Effects, and Undo History palettes are there.

Note: For help with Palette Bin contents, see "Using the Palette Bin" on page 59.

You can start with almost any project in this lesson, because they are independent of each other, in both subject matter and skill level.

Unless you're starting your work in this book here, you're already very familiar with the process of using the predefined Organizer tags (for Lessons and Project numbers) or the File Browser (using the Folders palette to select the Lessons\Lesson 8 folder) to locate and open files. This process is described in detail in Lesson 2, so we won't describe the detail for the projects in this lesson. Lesson 8 also requires some file structures, custom tags, and skills covered in Lessons 1 and 2.

Project 1: Copying from one image into another

A stunningly simple way to combine part of one image with another is to use the familiar Copy and Paste commands. Your goal in this little project is to create a more spectacular fireworks display by borrowing bursts from a couple of photographs and pasting these into another.

1 Using either Organizer or the File Browser, find and open the 08_01a, 08_01b, and 08_01c files (three photos of fireworks) in Standard Edit.

2 Select the Lasso tool (⌇) in the toolbox and the 08_01b thumbnail in the Photo Bin to make it active.

Note: You can use the Elliptical Marquee tool instead of the Lasso tool to create selections. If you do so, you may need to zoom out or drag the selection shape into place around the burst.

3 Drag the Lasso tool around the single burst in the image. Keep the selection reasonably close to the outer edge of the burst, but don't even think about trying to be precise.

(If necessary, you can select Add To Selection (⬚) or Subtract From Selection (⬚) in the tool options bar, and then drag around the small areas you want to add or subtract from the first selection.)

4 Choose Edit > Copy, or press Ctrl + C.

5 Select the 08_01a thumbnail in the Photo Bin to make that image active, and choose Edit > Paste or press Ctrl + V.

6 Use the Move tool (⯬) to move, resize, and rotate the pasted-in layer so that it doesn't block the other bursts on the lower layer. When it looks right to you, click Commit (✔) in the tool options bar.

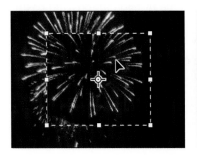 

7 Select the 08_01c thumbnail in the Photo Bin, and repeat Steps 3-6.

💡 *Try this: Hold down Alt and drag with the Move tool to simultaneously duplicate and move a selection or a layer. The burst in the lower left corner of the illustration above was created in this way from the burst pasted into the upper right corner; the newly duplicated layer was then rotated and resized.*

8 Save your work (File > Save) as a Photoshop (PSD) file named **08_01_Work** in the My CIB Work folder you created in the Lessons folder. Then close the file.

Wasn't that easy? You're already finished with this project, so you can close all the files without saving the changes.

Project 2: Placing two or more photographs in one file

Sometimes you don't especially want to get fancy, but you want to show several photographs side by side in a single image file. For example, you could include photographs of similar items that you want to sell on a web-based auction site or on your own web pages.

In this project, the photographs you'll use show two views of a river adventure trip: one showing the tranquil majesty of the setting, the other showing some white-water action.

Checking file compatibility

When you combine images, it's good to confirm that they are similar in size and resolution. Otherwise, the process may require additional steps or produce unsatisfactory results. This time, you won't use Organizer to locate and open the project files.

1 In Standard Edit, choose File > Browse Folders to open the File Browser.

2 In the File Browser, make sure that you can see the tabs for the Folders, Preview, and Metadata palettes.

• If you don't see any palettes, click Toggle Expanded View ( ) in the lower left corner.

• If the Folders and Metadata palettes are collapsed, double-click those tabs to expand the palettes.

3 In the Folders palette, find and select the Lesson 8 folder in the Lessons folder.

4 Click once to select—but not open—the 08_02a.jpg file (the image of the canyon). Look in the Metadata palette and write a note to yourself recording these values:

- Width (in pixels)
- Height (in pixels)
- Resolution (in pixels per inch)

5 Select the 08_02b.jpg file (the raft on the rapids) and write down the same Metadata values for that image.

Fortunately, the images have the same resolution, which means less work for you. Although the widths of the two images are identical, the heights are different.

6 Click and then Ctrl-click to select the thumbnails of these two image files. Then open both files at once by doing one of the following:

- Within the File Browser, choose File > Open.
- Right-click one of the selected thumbnails and choose Open on the context menu.

7 Close the File Browser (Window > File Browser).

Note: *For more information about image resolution and how to change it, see Photoshop Elements 3.0 Help.*

Cropping to synchronize the dimensions

In the previous procedure, you confirmed that the two images have the same resolution and widths, but their heights are different. How could this happen? Because one image came from a digital camera and the other is a scan of a film-based print.

Essentially, you have three choices: (1) to leave the images sized as they are; (2) to crop the larger photograph to match the height of the first image; or (3) to resize the larger photograph to match the height of the first image but not its width. In this procedure, you'll use method #2, using the dimensions of the smaller image, which you wrote down in the previous procedure (640 pixels by 428 pixels).

1 In the Photo Bin, select the 08_02a thumbnail.

2 Select the Crop tool ( ) in the toolbox.

3 In the tool options bar, type **640 px** (include the units) in Width and **428 px** in Height. If an error message appears about the dimensions, click OK, and then try typing again.

Note: The default units for Width and Height are inches, so it's important to include the **px** *with the value in each case. Otherwise, Photoshop Elements will attempt to generate an image the size of an ordinary sofa. This is not only not what you want for this project, it can also cause serious memory problems or even choke the application, depending on your computer memory capacity and settings.*

4 In the image window, drag the Crop tool diagonally across the image.

5 Drag the handles at the corners as needed to include as much of the picture as possible, but be careful to keep the crop boundary within the image area.

Regardless of how you drag the corners, the proportions of the crop area remain constant. That's because you set the relationship between width and height in Step 3.

6 Apply the crop in any one of the following ways:

• Double-click in the image window.

• Click Commit (✔) in the tool options bar.

• Choose Image > Crop.

• In the toolbox, double-click the Crop tool (⛏), and then click Crop in the message that appears.

7 In the tool options bar, select Clear.

Clicking the Clear button releases the Crop tool from the 640 by 428 width-to-height ratio that you defined in Step 3. Until you click Clear, this restriction continues to govern the Crop tool in later work sessions, regardless of what image file is active.

Keeping constant crop dimensions can be handy if you usually want to create the same-sized images for your work. However, it can be frustrating if you forget about it and try to drag a rectangle with a different width-to-height ratio.

Combining the pictures and resizing the canvas

Now that the pictures are equally sized, and you know that they have the same resolution, you can proceed to place both images in one file.

1 Arrange the two image windows so that you can see at least part of both images.

2 Select the Move tool (⊹).

3 Hold down Shift and drag the rafting photograph (08_02b) into the image window of the canyon photograph (08_02a). Carefully release the mouse button first and then the Shift key. You can close the 08_02b (rafting) file now.

As you can see in the Layers palette, the photographs are now stacked in separate layers. Only Layer 1 is visible: the picture of the raft going down the rapids.

4 Choose Image > Resize > Canvas Size.

5 In the Canvas Size dialog box, do the following:

• For Anchor, select the middle square in the left column.

• Select the Relative check box (to increase the canvas size by whatever Width and Height values you enter).

- In Width, type **100** and select percent.
- Click OK.

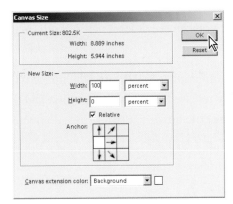

6 Hold down Shift and drag Layer 1 to the right until its edges align with the far edges of the canvas. (You may need to zoom out first.)

Holding down the Shift key as you drag constrains the movement so that the vertical position of the layer can't change.

7 Choose File > Save As. Name the image **08_02_Work**, and save it in Photoshop (PSD) format in the My CIB Work folder. Leave the file open for the next procedure.

Saving the file with JPEG compression

JPEG is a compression method that is ideal for bitmap images such as photographs. Currently, the size of the PSD work file has swollen considerably to almost 3 MB. It's time to see whether or not you can save space by saving the file as a JPEG.

1 Choose File > Save As.

2 In the Save As dialog box, choose JPEG on the Format pop-up menu. (It's not necessary to change the file name or location.) Then click Save.

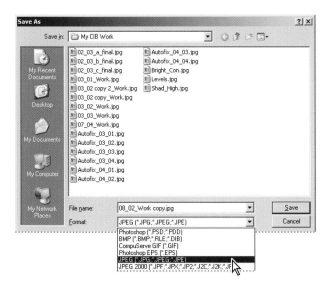

3 When the JPEG Options dialog box appears, drag the slider to set the Quality at 12. Notice the Size information for the file. Don't click OK yet.

4 Try different Quality settings and notice the changes in the file size and in the quality of the image in the image window (with Preview selected). Then click OK to save the file at the quality level you want.

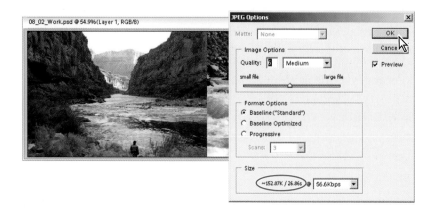

Note: It may be difficult to see any difference in the image quality at the current zoom level. You can select Cancel and go back to the original work file to increase the zoom so that you can see fine details. Then start again at Step 1.

5 Choose File > Browse Folders, and use the Folders palette to find and select the Lessons\My CIB Work folder.

6 Select the 08_02_Work.psd thumbnail (without opening the file) and note the File Size in the Metadata palette. Then select the 08_02_Work copy.jpg thumbnail and compare its file size to the PSD version of the file.

7 Choose File > Close All.

Even at Maximum quality, the conversion to JPEG format drastically reduces the file size without altering the viewing quality of the image.

Project 3: Erasing areas of image layers

In this project, you'll start with a Photoshop PSD file that we're prepared for you. In it, four photographs have been stacked in layers, each one blocking your view of the ones below it. Your goal is to erase—cut holes, so to speak—in each layer, allowing parts of the other layers to show through. You'll end up with a collage, piecing together the four fruits and vegetables into an equally divided image.

There are several ways to erase. One way is to use the Eraser tool, which replaces erased areas with the Background Color, just like a regular eraser removes pencil marks so that you can see the paper underneath. Another way is to use the Background Eraser tool, which replaces the erased area with transparent pixels, just like wiping wet paint off of a piece of glass. In either case, the process involves dragging the eraser over the area you want to remove.

In this project, you'll erase by selecting and then deleting entire areas of the various layers. This makes it easy to create sharp, precise boundaries between the four quarters of the final image.

Setting up a grid for precise selections

Knowing how to use rulers and grids is essential when you do precision work.

1 Using the File Browser or Organizer, open the 08_03.psd file (an artichoke).

2 Choose View > Rulers, and then choose View > Grid.

3 On the View menu, make sure that there is a check mark by the Snap To Grid command, or choose that command now.

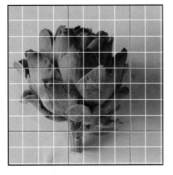

4 Choose Edit > Preferences > Grid, and then select the following:

- In Gridline Every, type **1** and select Inches in the pop-up menu.

- In Subdivisions, type **4**, if it is not already selected

- Click OK to close the Preferences dialog box.

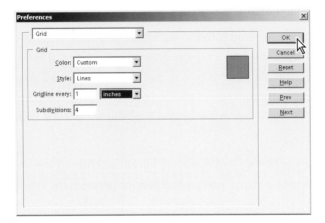

5 In the image window, drag the zero-point marker (the corner box where the two rulers intersect) to the center of the image, so that it snaps into place at the 1.25-inch marker on both rulers.

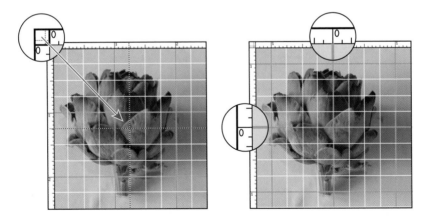

Now the 0, 0 position on the rulers is set at the center of the image.

6 Choose File > Save As. Name the file **08_03_Work.psd**, and save it in the Lessons\My CIB Work folder.

Erasing part of the top layer

This PSD file has four layers, which we created for you by dragging layers from several images into one file. Because the top layer covers the entire image area, all you can see is that layer—unless, of course, you peek at the Layers palette, where you can see thumbnails of all four layers.

1 In the Layers palette, select the top layer, Layer 3, showing the artichoke.

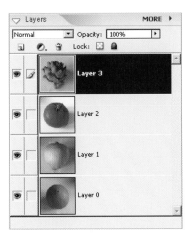

2 In the toolbox, select the Rectangular Marquee tool ( ).

3 Drag from the center of the image (0,0 point) to the upper left until the selection marquee snaps into place at the corner of the image.

4 Invert the selection (choose Select > Inverse or press Shift + Ctrl + I).

Now, everything except the first quadrant of the image is selected, and the upper left quadrant is protected from changing.

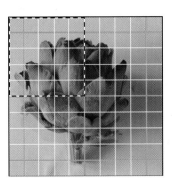 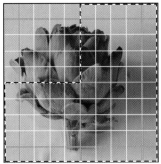

5 Choose Edit > Delete or press Delete.

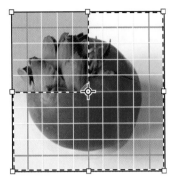

Do not deselect yet.

Erasing parts of lower layers in the image

By erasing three-quarters of the artichoke layer, Layer 3, you exposed three-quarters of the tomato, Layer 2, the next layer down. You'll uncover parts of the onion and orange layers by performing similar deletions.

Before you begin, make sure that the selection from the previous procedure is still active and that the Rectangular Marquee tool ([⬚]) is selected.

1 In the Layers palette, click the eye icon (👁) for Layer 3 (the artichoke) to hide it, and select Layer 2 (the tomato).

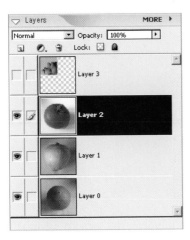

Note: It's not absolutely necessary to hide Layer 3, but it simplifies your view as you perform the next steps.

2 Choose Select > Inverse, so that only the upper left quadrant is selected. Then move the pointer inside the selection and drag it to the right until it snaps into place in the upper right corner of the image window.

Note: The shortcut for inverting a selection is Ctrl + Shift + I. You're going to invert numerous times in these steps, so this is a good chance to practice using it.

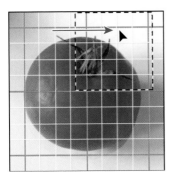

3 Invert the selection (Select > Inverse or press Ctrl + Shift + I) to select three-quarters of the tomato. Then press Delete (or choose Edit > Delete), revealing three-quarters of the underlying onion.

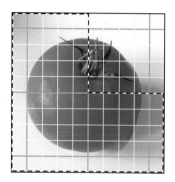 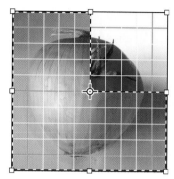

4 In the Layers palette, click the eye icon to hide Layer 2 (the tomato wedge).

5 Repeat the process to erase all but the lower left quadrant of the onion layer:

• Select Layer 1.

• Invert the selection and drag it to the lower left quadrant. Then invert the selection again.

• Press Delete.

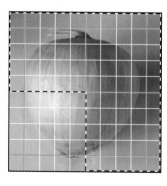 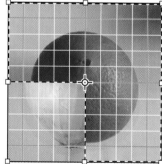

6 Choose View > Snap To Grid, to deselect that option.

Note: The Snap To Grid feature can interfere with other kinds of work, especially when you try to select areas that don't align to the grid.

Finishing and saving the project

You've done your erasing. It's time to see the overall results. You're also going to save your work twice: one work file and one JPEG file.

1 Choose View > Rulers and then View > Grid, to turn off these displays.

2 In the Layers palette, click to restore the eye icons for each of the four layers so that all are visible.

Because you've used the Snap To Grid feature and rulers to align your selections precisely, your final image has no gaps between the quadrants or uneven margins.

3 Choose File > Save. (This saves the latest changes to the 08_03_Work.psd file in the My CIB Work folder.)

4 Choose File > Save As.

5 In the Save As dialog box, select JPEG as the format, and click Save. (It is not necessary to change the file name or location.)

6 When the JPEG Options dialog box appears, drag the Quality slider to 12. (Notice the file-size information before you click OK.)

7 Close the file (choose File > Close or click Close (✕) on the image window).

JPEG format does not support layers, so creating a JPEG version of the image merges the layers into a single, flat image.

Congratulations! You've finished this project.

Now that you're done, can you think of another way to do this project? If you thought of the Cookie Cutter tool, you're right. It has a square shape option that you could use with the grid and rulers to cut out the quadrants directly rather than by inverting selections and deleting. For another example of using the Cookie Cutter, see "Project 4: Drawing a frame with the Custom Shape tool" on page 235.

Project 4: Using a gradient clipping path

Digital-graphics work consistently challenges you to strike a balance between flexibility and file size. Flexibility means the ability to go back and revise your work. In the previous project, the procedure gives priority to limiting the file size. If you wanted to go back and switch the positions of the artichoke and the tomato quadrants, you'd have to start from the beginning because those pixels are no longer in the final work file.

In this project, you'll give priority to flexibility. You'll apply a clipping layer to combine one image with another. Your final work file will contain all the original pixel information, so that you can go back later and make adjustments whenever needed.

Arranging the image layers

A clipping path is a layer that serves as a kind of cutting template for another layer. For example, text can be a clipping path, as if you glued an image onto the text and then dissolved all the areas of the image that weren't attached to the text characters. Whatever is transparent on the clipping path layer produces transparency on the image layer.

In this project, you're going to combine two views of a monument so that one forms the context for the other. You'll make the photograph of the statue gradually fade into the picture of the plaza, which will serve as a kind of frame for the image. How do you create such a transition? By using a clipping path that gradually flows from fully opaque to fully transparent pixels.

1 Using the File Browser or Organizer, open the 08_04a and 08_04b files (the plaza and statue).

2 Arrange the two image windows so that you can see at least some of both images (or choose Window > Images > Tile).

3 Select the Move tool (⤢). Then hold down Shift and drag from the statue image window (08_04b) into the plaza image window (08_04a). Release the mouse button when you see the dark outline around the plaza image, and then release the Shift key.

4 Close the 08_04b image window without saving the file.

5 In the Layers palette, select Layer 1 (the statue). Then choose Image > Resize > Scale.

6 In the tool options bar, type **65%** in the W (width) option, and then click Maintain Aspect Ratio ( ) to scale the height by the same percentage.

7 Click Commit (✔) in the tool options bar to accept the changes.

Setting up work files with a saved selection

You'll do two versions of this project, both of which require the same selection. By making that selection once and then creating the duplicate file, you save time and effort.

1 In the Layers palette, click the eye icon (◉) for the Background layer to hide it, but leave Layer 1 selected (the statue image).

2 Select the Magic Wand tool (✎), click the transparent area (shown as a checkerboard) around the image. Then choose Select > Inverse, or press Ctrl + Shift I.

The selection now includes only the visible part of the layer.

3 Choose Select > Save Selection, and name the selection **Statue** before you click OK in the Save Selection dialog box.

4 In the Layers palette, click New Layer (▣) to create and select a new, blank layer named Layer 2.

5 Choose File > Duplicate, and accept the default name (08_04a Copy) by clicking OK in the dialog box that appears.

6 Minimize the duplicate file (click the Minimize button on the far right of the window title bar) and make the original file (08_04a) active.

Now you're all set up for both versions of the project.

Adding a gradient layer

You've used gradients in earlier lessons in this book, such as to create a sky in a Lesson 6 project. In that case, the color selections for the gradient were critical to the success of the project. In this case, the color is irrelevant; only the opacity of the gradient will make a difference to the final result.

1 In the Layers palette, hide Layer 1 (the statue) by clicking its eye icon (👁). Keep Background also hidden so that all you see is the selection marquee and the checkerboard pattern indicating transparency.

Note: If the selection is no longer active, choose Select > Load Selection. Click OK in the dialog box to load the Statue selection.

2 In the toolbox, select the Gradient tool (▬), and then select the Default Foreground And Background Colors icon, or press D.

3 In the tool options bar, click the arrow to open the Gradient Editor, and select the Foreground To Transparent thumbnail. Click anywhere outside the Gradient Editor to close it.

4 Make sure that the other settings in the tool options bar are as follows:

- Linear Gradient (▭)
- Normal for Mode
- 100% for Opacity
- Transparency (selected)

5 Drag the Gradient tool vertically, beginning slightly below the top of the selection area and dragging at least three-fourths of the way to the bottom of the selection area.

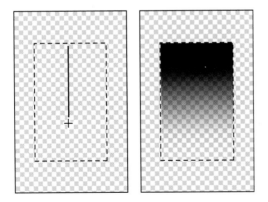

Note: It is not necessary to begin a gradient at the top of the selection or to end it at the bottom. You can even start and end the gradient outside the image boundaries.

6 Choose Select > Deselect, or press Ctrl + D to deselect the gradient area.

When you create a gradient clipping path for your own projects, you do not have to use a selection. Or, you can use one you create with selection tools.

Applying the clipping path to a layer

With your gradient layer completed, it's time to put it to work.

1 In the Layers palette, drag the new gradient layer (Layer 2) under Layer 1 (the statue).

2 Click to set eye icons (👁) so that all three layers are visible.

3 Select Layer 1 (the top layer in the stack) and choose Layer > Group With Previous.

Note: This action defines Layer 2 as the clipping path for Layer 1. In the Layers palette, Layer 1 is indented and shows an arrow (↴) pointing down to Layer 2.

4 Choose File > Save As.

5 In the Save As dialog box, name the file **08_04_Work**, and save it in the My CIB Work folder, selecting Photoshop (PSD) for the Format.

💡 *Another way to group layers is to hold down Alt and move the pointer between the two layers. When the pointer appears as two overlapping circles (⬬), click.*

Creating a painted clipping path

You don't have to use a gradient as a clipping path. You can use vector shapes, such as text or layers that you create with a shape tool. Or, you can use free-form shapes with feathery edges, which is what you'll do next.

In this procedure, you'll work with the Brush tool, which works like a versatile adjustable paintbrush to apply color.

1 In the Photo Bin, select the 08_04a Copy thumbnail to make that image window active.

2 Select the Brush tool (✎), and then select Soft Round 27 in the tool options bar.

Note: Be careful to select the Brush tool, not the Selection Brush tool, which has a different function.

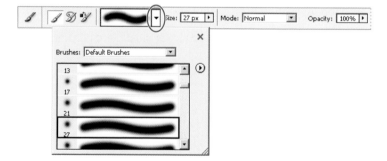

3 Choose Select > Load Selection, and make sure the Statue saved selection appears in the dialog box before you click OK.

4 In the Layers palette, select Layer 2, if necessary, and then paint in the image window, covering the upper part of the statue, as shown in the illustration below.

Note: The Brush tool paints with the Foreground Color selected in the toolbox. When you intend to use the painted areas as a clipping path, it's not important what that color is— any 100%-opacity color will do equally well. (The illustrations here and on the following pages use bright magenta paint so that you can see the action easily.)

5 Drag Layer 1 (the statue image) to the top of the layer stack, and choose Layer > Group With Previous.

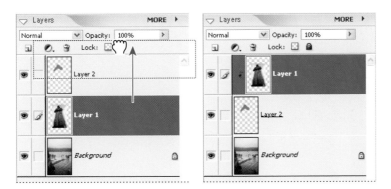

Now the statue appears only in the areas that you painted in Step 4.

Refining the results

There are a few more things you can do to change the results you've achieved so far. Even though Layer 2 (the painted clipping path) is no longer visible by itself, you can continue to paint on it, which will affect the statue image.

1 Select Layer 2 in the Layers palette, and make sure that the selection marquee is still active in the image window.

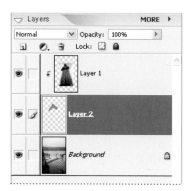 

2 Drag the paint brush below the visible part of the statue to reveal more of the statue.

3 In the tool options bar, reduce the Opacity of the paint to about 30%. Drag the paint brush around the outside of the visible area of the statue to make that area of the statue layer partly visible.

4 Choose Select > Deselect.

5 With Layer 2 still selected, click the empty box next to the eye icon for Layer 1 to link these two layers. An icon ( ) appears, reminding you that Layer 1 is linked to the currently selected layer (Layer 2).

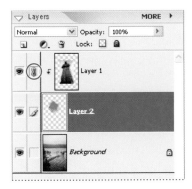

6 Select the Move tool ( ), and drag the layer up and to one side of the image. Then hold down Shift (to constrain the proportions) and drag one of the corner anchor points to resize the statue layer and the clipping path layer simultaneously. When you have adjusted the statue to your satisfaction, click Commit (✔) in the tool options bar.

7 Choose File > Save As, and save the file in the My CIB Work folder as **08_04 Copy_Work.psd**.

Congratulations, you've completed another project. In this one, you've used two methods of creating a clipping-path layer from a blank layer: by applying a Foreground To Transparent gradient and by painting a limited area of an empty layer. You've also delved into clipping paths (grouped layers), where the opaque pixels in one layer do not themselves appear in the image but instead determine which pixels on a different layer are visible. You've also practiced your layer-management and selection skills, and learned how to link layers so that you can transform them as one without merging them.

Saving and organizing your finished files

If you've already finished earlier lessons in this book, you are familiar with this final phase of the lesson. You're going to add tags to the work files, which were already added to the Organizer when you saved them, thanks to the Include In Organizer option in the Save As dialog box.

1 Click Photo Browser (⌐▦) on the Photoshop Elements Editor shortcuts bar to switch to Organizer. If Back To All Photos appears above the thumbnails area, select it.

2 Choose Find > Untagged Items.

3 Choose Edit > Select All or press Ctrl + A to select all the thumbnails.

4 Drag the Work Files tag and Lesson 8 tags to the thumbnails to apply them.

5 Select the two thumbnails of your Project 4 work files and choose Edit > Stack > Stack Selected Photos.

6 Repeat Step 5 to stack the JPEG and PSD versions of your vegetable-fruit collage work files. Do this one more time for your river-rafting work files.

You can now select Back To All Photos to see the entire catalog of thumbnails.

Can you believe it?—you've finished this project, this lesson, and this entire Classroom in a Book. Congratulations!

Learning more

We hope you've gained confidence, skill, and knowledge about how to use Photoshop Elements 3.0 for your digital photography work. But this book is just the start. The goal until now has been for you to find your way around the work area and gain skills in using a few representative tools, commands, palettes, and features. There's much more to be explored that's beyond the scope of this introductory book.

At this point, you probably feel comfortable trying new techniques and using the tools, menus, palettes, and options. You can learn even more by studying the Photoshop Elements 3.0 Help system, which is built into the application (choose Help > Photoshop Elements 3.0 Help). Also, don't forget to look for tutorials, tips, and expert advice on the Adobe website, www.adobe.com.

Review questions

1 What are some of the visual aids you can turn on to help you position items precisely in an image window.

2 How can you customize a grid or ruler?

3 Can you describe the differences between deleting part of an image layer with the Background Eraser tool and with the Delete key?

4 What is a clipping path and how do you create it? What are grouped layers?

5 What is the purpose of the blank boxes next to the eye icons on the Layers palette?

Review answers

1 Using the View menu, you can choose the Rulers and Grid commands to toggle them on and off. The Rulers appear on the left and upper sides of the image window. The grid is superimposed on the image. Neither of these elements is a permanent part of the image, and neither appears when you print the image or save it in another format, such as JPEG.

2 You can customize grids and rulers using the Preferences dialog box (choose Edit > Preferences > Units And Rulers or Edit > Preferences > Grid). You can also choose View > Snap To Grid. When selected, this command makes items snap into alignment with the nearest grid lines when you move them with the Move tool.

3 You must make a selection in the image window before the Delete key will erase the selected area on the selected layer. This is not necessary with the Background Eraser tool. The Delete key erases everything within the selected area, and does so completely. The Background Eraser tool deletes only the areas over which you drag. You can change the size and shape of the tool and its opacity, so that it erases only partially.

4 *Clipping path* and *grouped layers* are synonyms in Photoshop Elements 3.0. The lower of the two grouped layers must have areas of transparency. The other layer must be directly above it and must be selected. Choose Layer > Group With Previous to create the clipping path. When this is done, the transparent areas of the lower layer also apply to the upper one. Effectively, the layer with the transparency serves as a cut-out form for the other layer—and that's all it does.

5 When you select a layer, an icon (usually a brush) fills the box as a reminder that the layer is active. When you click the empty box for a layer, it links the layer to the active layer. You can then move and transform the two layers as a unit without merging them.

Index